Real-Life Math

Fractions, Ratios, and Rates

by
Tom Campbell

illustrated by Lois Leonard Stock

J. WESTON
WALCH
PUBLISHER

Portland, Maine

Dedication

To Lori

User's Guide
to
Walch Reproducible Books

As part of our general effort to provide educational materials that are as practical and economical as possible, we have designated this publication a "reproducible book." The designation means that the purchase of the book includes purchase of the right to limited reproduction of all pages on which this symbol appears:

Here is the basic Walch policy: We grant to individual purchasers of this book the right to make sufficient copies of reproducible pages for use by all students of a single teacher. This permission is limited to a single teacher and does not apply to entire schools or school systems, so institutions purchasing the book should pass the permission on to a single teacher. Copying of the book or its parts for resale is prohibited.

Any questions regarding this policy or requests to purchase further reproduction rights should be addressed to:

Permissions Editor
J. Weston Walch, Publisher
321 Valley Street • P.O. Box 658
Portland, Maine 04104-0658

1   2   3   4   5   6   7   8   9   10
ISBN 0-8251-3812-4
Copyright © 1998
J. Weston Walch, Publisher
P. O. Box 658 • Portland, Maine 04104-0658
Printed in the United States of America

Contents

Ratios

How to Use This Series

The Real-Life Math series is a collection of handouts designed to put math into the context of real-world settings. This series contains math appropriate for prealgebra students all the way up to precalculus students. Problems can be used as reminders of old skills in new contexts, as an opportunity to show how a particular skill is used, or as an enrichment activity for stronger students. Because this is a collection of reproducibles, you may make as many copies of each handout as you wish.

Please be aware that this collection does not and cannot replace teacher supervision. Although formulas are often given on the student page, this does not replace teacher instruction on the subjects to be covered. Teaching notes include extension suggestions, many of which involve the use of outside experts. If it is not possible to get these presenters to come to your classroom, it may be desirable to have individual students contact them by phone or visit their office.

We have found a significant number of real-world settings for this collection, but it is not a complete list. Let your imagination go, and use your own experience or the experience of your students to create similar opportunities for contextual study.

Foreword

As a mathematician, I have to admit that I always used to greet the question, "When are we ever going to use this?" with some annoyance. It was obvious to me that students needed the material to do well on my tests and maybe in future classes. Admittedly, that doesn't give students, unless they really just love math, much on which to hang their hats. With greater experience, I began answering the question with esoteric phrases about how well math trains one's mind and why training the mind is the highest goal of a good education. Still, some students stare at me blankly, trying to find the "real" meaning of their math voyage.

Well, we really DO use math every day. Yes, sometimes it is just to balance a checkbook or make change, but in an incredible variety of professional and personal settings, we use math skills that were drilled into us without the slightest hint of a context. Once I started to think about all the areas of life where math and mathematical thought were central, I started having fun. I have talked with stockbrokers, restaurateurs, mechanics, haberdashers, contractors, baseball statisticians, bankers, carpet salespeople, and grocers to learn about how they use math each day. I hope that these activities will be as much fun for your students and provide them with as much contextual background as they have for me. As a teacher you will be amazed by how open professionals in other fields are to helping your students extend their understanding and grounding in learning math.

— T.E.C.
Portland, ME 1998

1. A Construction Site

Goal

To use adding and subtracting fractions in a construction setting

NCTM Standards Addressed

Standard 1: Mathematics as Problem Solving

Standard 2: Mathematics as Communication

Standard 4: Mathematical Connections

Standard 8: Geometry from an Algebraic Perspective

Standard 12 (MS): Geometry

Standard 13 (MS): Measurement

Teaching Notes

Many of us learned fractions for the first time by talking about cutting up pies and cakes. Almost immediately afterward, we were manipulating fractions without a context. The question "What is $\frac{1}{7} + \frac{3}{5}$?" has an answer, but not one we can place in context. Practicing addition and subtraction of fractions is easier for students if they have a good sense of what the fraction is "part of."

Context

Many of us have to work with at least some sense of fractions. Most rulers and measuring sticks are scaled in fractional parts of inches, not decimal parts. Consequently, a construction or refurbishment site is a terrific source of fraction problems.

Extension Activities

Ask students to measure out and draw a scale drawing of a room in their house. They should identify the location of furniture, rugs, and so on. Scale drawings make use of both ratios and fractions.

Answers

1. 9'5¹⁵⁄₁₆"
2. 12'11" × 10'½"
3. 4'1¾"
4. 4⁷⁄₁₆"
5. 5¼" × 3½"
6. 25'10½"
7. 2'11⅜"
8. 95⅛" (7'11⅛") × 51¼" (4'3¼")

1. A Construction Site

Rulers and measuring tapes are often divided into inches. Inches are sometimes broken into halves, quarters, eighths, tenths, or sixteenths depending on the measurer. The inches can also be grouped in sets of 12 into feet. Most measurements in the construction business are given in feet, inches, and fractions of inches.

Michael Macklin has a general contracting business. He and his employees always measure carefully to make sure they cut their materials correctly. On a recent job site, they encountered the following situations. Give Michael's crew a hand with the following measurements:

1. Michael is putting in a countertop. He is going to put the countertop flush against the wall on one end, and trim it with a board that is ⁵⁄₁₆" thick on the other end. If Michael wants the counter to end exactly 9'6½" from the wall, how long should he cut the countertop?

   _____

2. Michael has hired Matteen to build the deck. Matteen can just fit a deck that is 13'6" along the side of the house by 10'4" out from the house. The customer wants a railing; however, that will be 3½" wide, running around the three sides not attached to the house. What will be the dimensions of the "livable space" on the deck?

   _____

3. Michael has hired Sarah to build a square window frame out of wood that is ¾" thick. The dimensions need to be 4'3¼" square. If Sarah cuts the two sides of the square to be 4'3¼" long, how long should she cut the top and bottom pieces to fit between these two sides?

   _____

4. Lori has been hired to build the frame and outer walls of the house. The exterior walls will be made of ⅜"-dry wall, 3½"-wide studs, ¼"-thick exterior plywood, and ⁵⁄₁₆"-thick siding. How thick are the new walls altogether?

   _____

5. Michael's partner Rayhan is building a rectangular box out of ⅜"-thick wood as a curio shelf. He wants the box to be 6" long and 4¼" wide. If he insets the bottom into the box, to what dimensions should he cut the piece for the bottom?

   _____

(continued)

                   Real-Life Math: Fractions, Ratios, and Rates

1. A Construction Site *(continued)*

6. The house is 26'4¾" wide on the outside. Michael wants to cut his clapboards to fit the sides, but he knows that the corner trim covers 3⅛" in from the edge on each end. How long should he cut the clapboards?

_____

7. Concrete will be poured into forms at the job site tomorrow. The wall to be poured is to be 15'5⅜" long. Rayhan and Michael already have a form that is 12'6" long. How long should they make an additional form to make the wall the right length?

_____

8. Michael has asked Matteen to build a doorway for an existing door. Matteen knows that the door is 41¼" wide and 90⅜" tall. He knows the jamb will be 4¾" thick on the top and two sides of the doorway. What are the dimensions of the hole he should create in the wall to accommodate the doorjamb and the door?

_____

2. Selling Carpet

Goal

To learn about fractions and areas in the context of selling carpeting by the square yard

NCTM Standards Addressed

Standard 1: Mathematics as Problem Solving

Standard 2: Mathematics as Communication

Standard 4: Mathematical Connections

Standard 8: Geometry From an Algebraic Perspective

Standard 12 (MS): Geometry

Standard 13 (MS): Measurement

Teaching Notes

Students need to be familiar with conversions among yards, feet, and inches and with how to calculate the area of nonrectangular polygons with right-angle corners. The easiest way to do this is to break the shapes into consecutive rectangles, multiply sides to find their various areas, and then add these various areas.

Context

Most floor coverings are sold by the square yard. Carpeting in particular is priced this way. The shape of the original roll of carpet is not as important as the area of the actual room. Students may have lived in homes where carpeting was installed or may be interested in a sales position, such as that of a carpet salesperson.

Extension Activities

Ask students to measure several rooms in the school or at home in order to find the exact floor area of the space.

Answers

1. The Woodhouses should be charged $265.17.

2. The Khins should be charged $468.04.

3. The Traftons should be charged $353.05.

4. The Borduases should be charged $683.26.

5. The Spirers should be charged $1,188.24.

2. Selling Carpet

Phyllis's Carpet Warehouse has been installing office carpeting for years. They are now trying to break into the home carpeting business. When customers come into the salesroom, Phyllis asks them to bring an accurate floor plan of the room(s) to be carpeted. The staff can then calculate the square yardage of the floor to determine the price of the carpeting. Phyllis's prices include a 6-pound pad and installation, so customers have only one price to consider.

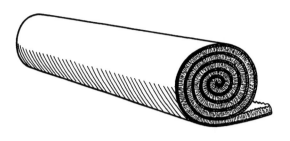

In the following situations, help Phyllis determine the price of the carpet installation:

1. The Woodhouse family is installing a playroom in their basement. They like the Berber carpet that is on sale for $12.99 a square yard. What price should be charged assuming the following floor plan is accurate?

Total cost: _____

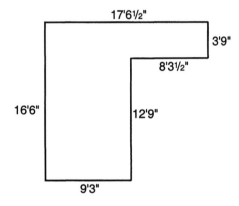

17'6½"

3'9"

8'3½"

16'6"

12'9"

9'3"

(continued)

2. **Selling Carpet** (continued)

2. The Khin family is carpeting their living room. They have chosen a deep-pile carpet that sells for $24.95 a square yard. How much should they be charged based on the following floor plan?

Total cost: _____

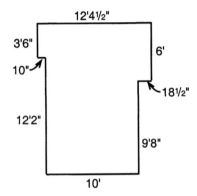

3. The Trafton family wants to install outdoor carpeting around their in-ground pool. The outdoor carpeting they have selected is $8.99 a square yard. How much should they be charged based on the following plan of the pool area?

Total cost: _____

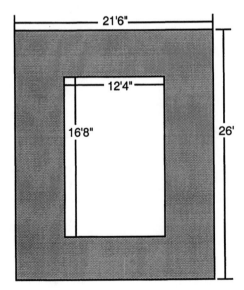

(continued)

2. Selling Carpet *(continued)*

4. The Borduas family is carpeting their dining room. They have chosen a low-pile carpet that sells for $18.75 a square yard. How much should they be charged based on the following floor plan?

Total cost: _____

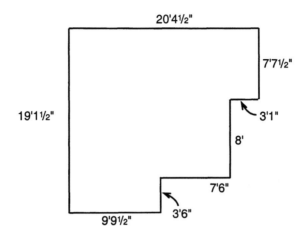

5. The Spirer family is carpeting their bedrooms. They have chosen a soft carpet that sells for $18.15 a square yard. How much should they be charged based on the following floor plans?

Total cost: _____

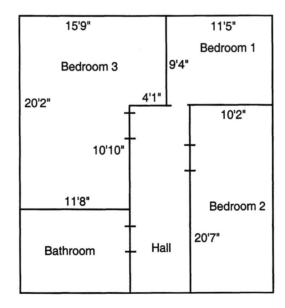

3. Sports Standings

Goal

To be able to read and create a chart of the standings in a sports conference or division

NCTM Standards Addressed

Standard 1: Mathematics as Problem Solving

Standard 2: Mathematics as Communication

Standard 3: Mathematics as Reasoning

Standard 4: Mathematical Connections

Standard 5: Algebra

Standard 6: Functions

Teaching Notes

Two columns in the following baseball and basketball standings are of interest (neither sport has ties, which change this procedure): Winning Percentage "PCT", which is the number of wins divided by the number of games played so far, and Games Behind "GB", which is the number of wins by Team A minus number of wins by team B, plus the number of losses by Team B minus number of losses by Team A. This sum is divided by two. If this result is positive, it is the number of games B is behind A, and if it is negative, the number of games A is behind B.

Context

Sports standings are not always as easy to figure out as they might appear. Placement in the table, with first place on the top, is usually based on "winning percentage." The GB, or "games behind" column contains either a whole number or a mixed number including ½. Sometimes (as in exercise 4) the first-place team is "behind" the second-place team because they have not played the same number of games.

Extension Activities

It is almost always baseball or basketball season. Have students use the newspaper to find standings and check their accuracy, or have students calculate the standings for your teams' leagues.

(continued)

3. Sports Standings *(continued)*

Answers

1. NBA Atlantic Division Standings 2/6/98

Team	W	L	PCT	GB
Miami	29	17	.630	-
New Jersey	27	21	.563	3
New York	25	21	.543	4
Washington	25	24	.510	5½
Orlando	23	25	.479	7
Boston	22	25	.468	7½
Philadelphia	14	31	.311	14½

2. NL West Final Standings 1988

Team	W	L	PCT	GB
Los Angeles	94	67	.584	-
Cincinnati	87	74	.540	7
San Diego	83	78	.516	11
San Francisco	83	79	.512	11½
Houston	82	80	.506	12½
Atlanta	54	106	.338	39½

3. National League Final Standings 1962

Team	W	L	PCT	GB
St. Louis	93	69	.574	-
Cincinnati	92	70	.568	1
Philadelphia	92	70	.568	1
San Francisco	90	72	.556	3
Milwaukee	88	74	.543	5
Los Angeles	80	82	.494	13
Pittsburgh	80	82	.494	13
Chicago	76	86	.469	17
Houston	66	96	.407	27
New York	53	109	.327	40

4. NBA Central Division Standings 1/30/98

Team	W	L	PCT	GB
Indiana	30	12	.714	½
Chicago	32	13	.711	-
Charlotte	28	17	.622	4
Atlanta	26	19	.578	6
Cleveland	25	20	.556	7
Milwaukee	22	21	.512	9
Detroit	20	23	.465	11
Toronto	10	34	.227	21½

NOTE: Indiana has the best winning percentage of the teams in this division, but because they have played fewer games, the formula for "games behind" puts them behind Chicago.

3. Sports Standings

Newspapers print the standings of various sports leagues daily. The team in first place is usually listed at the top. "First place" status is based on best "winning percentage," but "games behind" can also be used. Joe Gromelski is a sports editor for the *Lewiston Beacon*. He has to check the standings each day for accuracy (whether they are current or outdated).

Joe computes the winning percentage (PCT) by dividing the number of wins a team has by the number of games they have played. Joe then determines the games behind (GB) for each team. He subtracts a team's wins from the first place team's wins, then adds the team's losses to this difference. The next step is to subtract the first place team's losses. The resulting number is divided by two.

Help Joe with his job by filling in the PCT and the GB fields in the charts below.

1. NBA Atlantic Division Standings 2/6/98

Team	W	L	PCT	GB
Miami	29	17	_____	_____
New Jersey	27	21	_____	_____
New York	25	21	_____	_____
Washington	25	24	_____	_____
Orlando	23	25	_____	_____
Boston	22	25	_____	_____
Philadelphia	14	31	_____	_____

2. NL West Final Standings 1988

Team	W	L	PCT	GB
Los Angeles	94	67	_____	_____
Cincinnati	87	74	_____	_____
San Diego	83	78	_____	_____
San Francisco	83	79	_____	_____
Houston	82	80	_____	_____
Atlanta	54	106	_____	_____

(continued)

3. Sports Standings *(continued)*

3. National League Final Standings 1962

Team	W	L	PCT	GB
St. Louis	93	69	_____	_____
Cincinnati	92	70	_____	_____
Philadelphia	92	70	_____	_____
San Francisco	90	72	_____	_____
Milwaukee	88	74	_____	_____
Los Angeles	80	82	_____	_____
Pittsburgh	80	82	_____	_____
Chicago	76	86	_____	_____
Houston	66	96	_____	_____
New York	53	109	_____	_____

4. NBA Central Division Standings 1/30/98

Team	W	L	PCT	GB
Indiana	30	12	_____	_____
Chicago	32	13	_____	_____
Charlotte	28	17	_____	_____
Atlanta	26	19	_____	_____
Cleveland	25	20	_____	_____
Milwaukee	22	21	_____	_____
Detroit	20	23	_____	_____
Toronto	10	34	_____	_____

4. Cooking More Chili

Goal

To practice multiplication of fractions and conversion of measurements in the context of adjusting a recipe

NCTM Standards Addressed

Standard 1: Mathematics as Problem Solving

Standard 2: Mathematics as Communication

Standard 3: Mathematics as Reasoning

Standard 4: Mathematical Connections

Standard 5: Algebra

Standard 6: Functions

Standard 13 (MS): Measurement

Teaching Notes

Most recipe measures are given in mixed numbers. Adjusting and converting them to change the number of servings produced requires the multiplication or division of mixed numbers. Conversion of measurements (such as 16 tbsp = 1 cup and 6 tsp = 1 ounce) requires that students recognize the conversion factors and multiply or divide accurately.

Context

Restaurants and cooks frequently want to adjust a given recipe to produce enough servings for their needs. They have to multiply or divide the given measures by a factor that will give them enough servings.

Extension Activities

• Have students bring in favorite recipes and rework them for a different number of servings.

• Make a version of the converted recipe; it's real, and it's delicious. Just sauté the chopped vegetables in the oil, add all the tomato ingredients, spices, cashews, and raisins, and simmer over low heat for 90 minutes. Stir in vinegar just before serving.

Answers

Onions — 8¼ pounds; green peppers — 2¾ pounds; carrots — 2¾ pounds; celery — 22 stalks; vegetable oil — 1 cup + ½ tbsp; garlic — 11 cloves; canned tomatoes — 5½ quarts; kidney beans—5½-pound can; tomato sauce — 115½ ounces; tomato paste — 55 ounces; basil, cumin, salt — ½ cup + ¾ tsp (each); oregano — ½ cup + 1 tbsp + ½ tsp; chili powder — ¾ cup + 1¾ tbsp; bay leaves — 11; black pepper — 2 tbsp + ⅛ tsp; cashews — 2¾ pounds; raisins — 5½ cups; vinegar — 1⅜ cups.

4. Cooking More Chili

Andy and Billy have a bagel bakery and restaurant. They have decided to create a new vegetarian chili for their customers. In testing recipes, they make small amounts until they find one they like. In cooking for the restaurant, they will use a much bigger pot. The pot they have is 5½ times as big as the tester pot. They have decided on the recipe below. Use this recipe to create the version they should give to their chili cook. The conversion tables that follow the recipe will help you with your calculations.

Test Recipe Amounts	Ingredient	Full Recipe Amounts
1½ pounds	chopped onions	_____
½ pound	chopped green pepper	_____
½ pound	carrots	_____
4 stalks	chopped celery	_____
3 tbsp	vegetable oil	_____
2 large cloves	garlic	_____
1 quart	canned tomatoes	_____
16-ounce can	kidney beans	_____
21 ounces	tomato sauce	_____
10 ounces	tomato paste	_____
4½ tsp	basil	_____
1½ tbsp	cumin	_____
5 tsp	oregano	_____
1½ tbsp	salt	_____
2½ tbsp	chili powder	_____
2	bay leaves	_____

(continued)

4. Cooking More Chili *(continued)*

1¼ tsp	ground black pepper	_____
½ pound	raw cashew pieces	_____
1 cup	raisins	_____
¼ cup	cider vinegar	_____

Volume Conversion Table

1 gallon = 4 quarts = 8 pints = 16 cups = 128 fluid ounces
1 cup = 16 tablespoons = 48 teaspoons
1 fluid ounce = 2 tablespoons = 6 teaspoons
1 tablespoon = 3 teaspoons
1 pound = 16 ounces
1 liter = 1 cubic decimeter

5. Cooking Less Chili

Goal

To practice division of fractions and conversion of measurements in the context of adjusting a recipe

NCTM Standards Addressed

Standard 1: Mathematics as Problem Solving

Standard 2: Mathematics as Communication

Standard 3: Mathematics as Reasoning

Standard 4: Mathematical Connections

Standard 5: Algebra

Standard 6: Functions

Standard 13 (MS): Measurement

Teaching Notes

Most recipe measures are given in mixed numbers. Adjusting and converting them to change the number of servings produced requires the multiplication or division of mixed numbers. Conversion of measurements (such as 16 tbsp = 1 cup and 6 tsp = 1 ounce) requires that students recognize the conversion factors and multiply or divide accurately.

Context

Restaurants and cooks frequently want to adjust a given recipe to produce enough servings for their needs. They have to multiply or divide the given measures by a factor that will give them enough servings.

Extension Activities

• Have students bring in favorite recipes and rework them for a different number of servings.

• Make a version of the converted recipe; it's real, and it's delicious. Just sauté the chopped vegetables in the oil, add all the tomato ingredients, spices, cashews, and raisins, and simmer over low heat for 90 minutes. Stir in vinegar just before serving.

Answers

Onions — ½ pound; green peppers — 2⅔ ounces; carrots — 2⅔ ounces; celery — 1⅓ stalks; vegetable oil — 1 tbsp; garlic — ⅔ of a large clove; canned tomatoes — 10⅔ ounces; kidney beans — 5⅓-ounce can; tomato sauce — 7 ounces; tomato paste — 3⅓ ounces; basil, cumin, salt — ½ tbsp (each); oregano — 1⅔ tsp; chili powder — 2½ tsp.; bay leaves — ⅔ of a leaf; black pepper — ½ tsp; cashews — 2⅔ ounces; raisins — ⅓ cup; vinegar — 4 tsp.

5. Cooking Less Chili

Andy and Billy have a bagel bakery and restaurant. They have decided to sell their vegetarian chili recipe to their customers. Initially, when they created their tester recipe for the restaurant, they used a pot that was three times as big as the average pot that customers might use. Using the following ingredient list, create the smaller recipe that they could sell to their customers. The conversion tables that follow the recipe will help with your calculations. If necessary, round to the nearest ¼ tsp.

Test Recipe Amounts	Ingredient	Customer Recipe Amounts
1½ pounds	chopped onions	_____
½ pound	chopped green pepper	_____
½ pound	carrots	_____
4 stalks	chopped celery	_____
3 tbsp	vegetable oil	_____
2 large cloves	garlic	_____
1 quart	canned tomatoes	_____
16-ounce can	kidney beans	_____
21 ounces	tomato sauce	_____
10 ounces	tomato paste	_____
4½ tsp	basil	_____
1½ tbsp	cumin	_____
5 tsp	oregano	_____
1½ tbsp	salt	_____
2½ tbsp	chili powder	_____
2	bay leaves	_____

(continued)

5. Cooking Less Chili *(continued)*

1¼ tsp   ground black pepper   _____

½ pound   raw cashew pieces   _____

1 cup   raisins   _____

¼ cup   cider vinegar   _____

Volume Conversion Table

1 gallon = 4 quarts = 8 pints = 16 cups = 128 fluid ounces
1 cup = 16 tablespoons = 48 teaspoons
1 fluid ounce = 2 tablespoons = 6 teaspoons
1 tablespoon = 3 teaspoons
1 pound = 16 ounces
1 liter = 1 cubic decimeter

6. Miles Per Hour

Goal

To learn how to calculate the familiar rate of speed "miles per hour" (mph) from other measures of time, distance, and speed

NCTM Standards Addressed

Standard 1: Mathematics as Problem Solving

Standard 2: Mathematics as Communication

Standard 4: Mathematical Connections

Standard 10: Statistics

Standard 13 (MS): Measurement

Teaching Notes

The rate mph is used to measure speed, but seldom does it mean exactly 1 mile or exactly 1 hour. By using conversion factors, students can convert other speeds to miles per hour. Mph is usually a measure of average speed. If a sprinter runs 100 yards in 9.9 seconds, we calculate that he has gone 20.7 mph. However, since such races are run from a standing start, the sprinter probably reached a top speed of significantly more than 25 mph at some point during the race. Without a radar gun, we can calculate only the runner's average speed for the distance.

Context

Although mph is generally used on roads and highways, we also use it to describe the speed at which many objects travel.

Extension Activities

• Have students look up a record from the Olympics, where the time as well as the distance run, skated, skied, or ridden is given. Have them calculate the average speed of the racer.

• Allow students to conjecture about why average speed rises from short- to medium-length races and then falls again for longer races. (The rise is probably due to the impact of how long the racer takes to attain top speed and the falloff due to stamina.)

Answers

1. Coe averaged 17.6 mph for the race.

2. Meagher averaged 3.9 mph for the race.

3. Griffith Joyner averaged 21 mph for the race.

4. Johnson's pitch takes .41 seconds to get to the plate.

5. The linebacker averaged 17.8 mph for the 40-yard dash.

6. Gordon's race lasted 3.66 hours or 3 hours, 39 minutes, 27.5 seconds.

7. Kariuki averaged 13.8 mph for the race.

8. Iso-Hollo averaged 12.2 mph for the "extra-long" race.

6. Miles Per Hour

Lori is fascinated by the speed athletes can achieve. She has investigated many sports and enjoys using times and distances to calculate speed. Lori has carefully researched a variety of races and recorded speeds in sports in an effort to calculate time, distance, or speed.

To determine these rates Lori uses the formula d/t = s (distance divided by time equals speed). Lori likes to express her answers in miles per hour (mph) so she uses the conversion chart below to change her data into miles and hours before she does her computation. Can you help Lori with these calculations?

Conversion Factors

English Length	Metric Length
1 inch	= 2.54 centimeters
.394 inches	= 1 centimeter
1 foot	= 30.48 centimeters
.033 feet	= 1 centimeter
1 yard	= .9144 meters
1.094 yards	= 1 meter
1 mile	= 1.609 kilometers
.622 miles	= 1 kilometer

Volume

33.8 ounces	= 1 liter
1 ounce	= .03 liters

Temperature

Fahrenheit	Celsius

Fahrenheit degrees = ⅝ × (Celsius degrees) + 32

Comparative Measures

Distance

1 mile = 1,760 yards = 5,280 feet = 63,360 inches

1 yard = 3 feet = 36 inches

1 foot = 12 inches

1 kilometer = 1,000 meters = 100,000 centimeters = 1,000,000 millimeters

1 meter = 100 centimeters

1 centimeter = 10 millimeters

(continued)

6. Miles Per Hour *(continued)*

1. In 1981, Sebastian Coe of Great Britain ran 800 meters in a then-world record time of 1 minute, 41.73 seconds. What was his average speed in mph (to the nearest tenth) for the entire race?

   _____

2. Also in 1981, Mary T. Meagher of the United States swam 100 meters (using the butterfly stroke) in 57.93 seconds. What was her average speed in mph for the race?

   _____

3. In the 1988 Olympics in Seoul, Korea, Florence Griffith Joyner set a world record by running 200 meters in 21.34 seconds. What was her average speed in mph for the race?

   _____

4. Randy Johnson is one of the best pitchers of the current baseball era. His pitches have been clocked by radar at 101 mph. The ball travels 60' 6" from the pitcher's mound to home plate. How long does the ball take to get to the batter?

   _____

5. Football scouts often time players in the 40-yard dash, which is a measure of both quickness and speed. You might hear that a linebacker "runs a 4.6 40," which means he ran the 40-yard dash in 4.6 seconds. What was his average speed in mph for the dash?

   _____

6. Jeff Gordon, a top NASCAR driver, recently averaged 136.7 mph for a 500-mile race. How much time passed from the start of the race to the end?

   _____

7. In 1988, Julius Kariuki of Kenya set the Olympic 3,000-meter steeplechase in a record time of 8:05.51. What was his average speed in mph for the race?

   _____

8. In 1932, Volmari Iso-Hollo of Finland won the gold in the 3,000-meter steeplechase in 10:33.4. It was later discovered that the race was one lap too long, and Iso-Hollo actually ran 3,450 meters. What was his average speed in mph for the race?

   _____

7. Miles Per Gallon

Goal

To learn how to calculate the familiar rate "miles per gallon" (mpg) in purchasing or caring for a car

NCTM Standards Addressed

Standard 1: Mathematics as Problem Solving

Standard 2: Mathematics as Communication

Standard 4: Mathematical Connections

Standard 5: Algebra

Teaching Notes

Calculating mpg is a straightforward division problem: miles per gallon = miles driven/gallons of gas burned. Most students use it daily to project costs, diagnose mechanical problems, and recognize the value of more fuel-efficient cars—whether they realize that's what they're doing, or not!

Context

One consideration in buying and owning a car is its gas mileage. Because of the cost of gas, cars that can go farther on a gallon of gas cost less to own. Also, mpg fluctuates based on how the car is driven, with highway miles requiring less gas than miles driven in traffic. However, if a car's mpg changes while the type of driving remains the same, it may indicate a problem with the car's mechanical operations.

Extension Activities

• Ask students to determine the mpg for their own or their family's cars. Collect the data and make a classwide chart. Make predictions about types and sizes of cars and what kind of gas mileage they might get.

• Have students estimate the miles a car might be driven in a year (the national average is 15,000 miles) and figure out how much it will cost to buy the gas for a given car for a year.

Answers

1. Noemi's car got 29.0 mpg.

2. Tyler's favorite stock car is getting 5.2 mpg.

3. Valli's Land Rover got 24 mpg for the trip.

4. Ryan had driven 337 miles.

5. Mikel should see a mechanic. He got only 16.5 mpg on his trip, well below normal.

6. Caryn and Jemal can go 330 miles on a tank of gas.

7. Miles Per Gallon

"Gas mileage" is a selling point for many cars. It is a rate of how many miles the car will go on a gallon of gas. This number is different for "highway" driving and "city" driving, so it is more accurate to test your own car with your typical driving style. You do not need to burn exactly 1 gallon of gas to calculate "miles per gallon" (mpg). Just fill your car's tank full, write down your odometer reading, drive around for a few days, and then refill your car (full). Use your odometer to figure out how many miles you drove and the gas receipt to know how many gallons the car used. Divide the number of miles you drove by the number of gallons your car used. This will give you your "gas mileage" for that period of driving.

Help the following individuals calculate their gas mileage.

1. Noemi has had her car for a while and knows that it gets pretty good gas mileage. On a recent business trip she used 16.25 gallons of gas and drove 471 miles. To the nearest tenth of a mile, what was her gas mileage?

   _____

2. Tyler loves to watch stock-car racing. He figures that his favorite driver burns 115 gallons of fuel in a 600-mile race. What gas mileage is the stock car getting (to the nearest tenth of a gallon)?

   _____

3. Valli has a new Land Rover. On a recent trip she drove 450 miles and used 18.75 gallons of gas. What was her gas mileage?

   _____

4. Ryan has a computer in his car that tells him how far he has gone on a trip, how many gallons of gas he has used, and what his gas mileage is. Unfortunately, the buttons are stuck and after a recent trip he couldn't figure out how far he had traveled. He did know that he had averaged 29.3 miles per gallon and burned 11.5 gallons of gas. How long was the trip?

   _____

5. Mikel's car usually gets 28 miles per gallon in mostly highway driving. On a recent long trip mostly on highways, he used 14.2 gallons of gas for 234 miles. Should he see a mechanic to check if his car is working okay?

   _____

6. Caryn and Jemal have a new minivan. The van has a 15-gallon tank and gets 22 miles to the gallon. How far can the van go on a tank of gas?

   _____

8. Earned Run Average

Goal

To put the concept of rates into a sports context (earned run average) that is familiar to students

NCTM Standards Addressed

Standard 1: Mathematics as Problem Solving

Standard 2: Mathematics as Communication

Standard 4: Mathematical Connections

Standard 6: Functions

Standard 10: Statistics

Teaching Notes

A rate is usually an amount of work accomplished in a given period. It is given as "miles per hour" or "goals per game." Some rates, however, are stated differently. "Dollars per pound" is a rate, but "pound" isn't a period of time. Still other rates don't even use the word "per." In baseball, a pitcher's "earned run average" (ERA) is really a rate. It tells you the rate at which the pitcher gives up earned runs per game. ERA is calculated by dividing the number of innings a pitcher has pitched by nine to get the number of games pitched. You then take the earned runs the pitcher has yielded and divide by the number of games pitched to learn the ERA. The formula for ERA is

ERA = Runs /(Innings Pitched ÷ 9).

Context

The questions in this section were all researched using the *Baseball Encyclopedia*. Most baseball fans love to discuss and manipulate statistics, and ERA is one of the statistics that many fans don't understand.

Extension Activities

The *Baseball Encyclopedia* is an excellent resource for baseball statistics, going back more than a century. Encourage students to search this book, a current newspaper, or even get statistics on a school team to prepare several questions like those included in the handout.

Answers

1. Gibson's amazing 1968 ERA was 1.12.

2. Seaver's 1974 "worst" ERA was 3.20.

3. Rixey yielded 59 earned runs in 1916.

4. Podres pitched 196⅓ innings in 1957.

5. Young's career ERA was 2.63.

6. Beck yielded 47 runs in 1934.

7. The Forsch brothers' combined ERA for 1977 was 3.27.

Name _____   Date _____

8. Earned Run Average

Marc works for a baseball statistics company and has moved up to head of research. He has asked his employees to research earned run average (ERA) for him, and they have found some interesting statistics. The ERA tells you the rate at which the pitcher gives up earned runs per game. It is calculated using the formula: ERA = Runs/(Innings Pitched ÷ 9). Unfortunately, Marc has a new employee who doesn't always get ALL the information. Help Marc calculate the full information in the following situations:

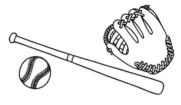

1. In 1968, Bob Gibson of the St. Louis Cardinals had his greatest season. He pitched 304⅔ innings and gave up only 38 runs. What was his ERA for the 1968 season ?

   _____

2. In 1974, Tom Seaver of the New York Mets had his worst season to that point in his career. He pitched 236 innings and gave up 84 runs. What was his ERA for the 1974 season ?

   _____

3. In 1916, Hall of Famer Eppa Jephtha Rixey had his finest season. He won 22 games for the Phillies and had an ERA of 1.85. Figure out how many earned runs Rixey yielded if he pitched 287 innings that year.

   _____

4. Johnny Podres was a star pitcher for the Dodgers, both in Brooklyn and Los Angeles. In 1957, he had an ERA of 2.66 while giving up 58 runs. How many innings did he pitch?

   _____

5. Denton True "Cy" Young was perhaps the greatest pitcher of all time. In his career, he pitched 7,356 innings and gave up 2,150 runs. What was his career ERA?

   _____

6. Walter "Boom-Boom" Beck had a tough year with the Brooklyn Dodgers in 1934. He had a 7.42 ERA in 57 innings. How many earned runs did he yield?

   _____

7. Brothers Ken and Bob Forsch both pitched in the National League in 1977. Bob was 20-7 with the Cardinals, yielding 84 runs in 217 innings. Ken was 5-8 with the Astros, yielding 26 earned runs in 86 innings. What was their combined ERA for the season?

   _____

9. Currency Trading

Goal

To learn about conversion rates in the context of international currency trading

NCTM Standards Addressed

Standard 1: Mathematics as Problem Solving

Standard 2: Mathematics as Communication

Standard 4: Mathematical Connections

Standard 5: Algebra

Standard 6: Functions

Teaching Notes

Currencies are traded in the open market every day. The prices are monitored in ratio to one another. As of January 30, 1998, for instance, it took $1.4556 Canadian to purchase $1.0000 U.S. It therefore cost $0.6870 U.S. to purchase $1.0000 Canadian. These ratios could be used to convert with another currency or perhaps to discover how much something costs in one place based on what it costs in another.

Context

Most financial reports include "how the dollar is doing against the yen (or deutsche mark)." A "strong dollar" (which can buy more yen) means that Americans can afford to buy more imports from Japan, whereas a "weak dollar" means the Japanese can afford more U.S. exports. International travelers also need to know conversions to get a sense of the value of their purchases.

Extension Activities

Most financial newspapers have a currency trading report. Ask students to convert between various currencies or determine prices for items in other currencies.

Answers

1. Jack would pay $7,877.12 (U.S.) for 1,000,000 yen.

2. Jack's 10,000,000 Mexican pesos can buy 1,744,378.75 Swiss francs.

3. A deutsche mark will buy 1.1275 guilders at this rate.

4. A U.S. dollar will buy 1,806.0 Italian lire.

5. The room cost Jack $171.52 (U.S.) per night.

6. Because 240 francs is the equivalent of 23.95 pounds, the Paris hat was cheaper.

7. A Swiss franc bought 121.95 Italian lire.

9. Currency Trading

Jack Markell is a currency trader for First National Bank of Chicago. Each day, he decides how to trade the cash money he has for currencies from other countries in an effort to turn a profit. Jack monitors currency prices in ratio to one another. As of January 30, 1998, for example, it took $1.4556 Canadian dollars to purchase $1.00 U.S. dollar. Jack determines the amount of U.S. dollars needed to purchase one Canadian dollar by dividing $1.00 U.S./ $1.4556 Canadian = .6870 U.S. To make profitable trades, Jack needs to know the conversion rates between the various countries at all times. Jack also recently went on a trip to Europe to visit with some of his trading partners. He had to do transactions in the money of each of the countries he visited.

Answer these questions about currency trading and conversion that Jack has encountered recently:

1. One U.S. dollar buys 126.95 Japanese yen on today's market. How many U.S. dollars would it cost Jack to buy 1,000,000 yen?

   _____

2. Jack learns that a Swiss franc is worth 5.7327 Mexican pesos. Jack has 10,000,000 Mexican pesos. How many Swiss francs can he buy?

   _____

3. Jack knows that a Dutch guilder will buy 0.8869 German deutsche marks. How many guilders will a deutsche mark buy?

   _____

4. Italian lire are smaller denominations than most currency. One Canadian dollar will buy 1240.70 lire. A Canadian dollar will also buy .6870 U.S. dollars. How many lire will one U.S. dollar buy?

   _____

5. The first stop on Jack's trip was London. His travel agent had booked him into a hotel for 105 pounds a night. How much did Jack pay for the room in U.S. dollars if 1 pound buys 1.6335 U.S. dollars?

   _____

6. Jack's next stop was in Paris. He saw a hat in a shop window there that was exactly like one he had nearly bought in London. In England the hat cost 25 pounds. In Paris, they were asking 240 francs. Jack knew that the franc was worth 0.09979 pounds. Which hat was a better deal?

   _____

7. Finally, Jack visited Zurich, Switzerland. He had decided not to go to Italy, so he needed to exchange his 100,000 lire for Swiss francs. The clerk handed him 820 francs. How many lire did 1 franc buy?

   _____

     Real-Life Math: Fractions, Ratios, and Rates

10. Heating Degree Days

Goal

To learn how averages are used in calculating a rate used in weather statistics

NCTM Standards Addressed

Standard 1: Mathematics as Problem Solving

Standard 2: Mathematics as Communication

Standard 4: Mathematical Connections

Standard 5: Algebra

Standard 6: Functions

Standard 10: Statistics

Standard 13 (MS): Measurement

Teaching Notes

On any given day, the average of the high and low temperatures is calculated. This average is subtracted from 65 to get the heating degree days for that date.

Context

Calculating heating degree days originated shortly after World War II; 65° F was picked as the temperature that people would want for their homes. Not only are heating degree days used in the northern winters, but cooling degree days (calculated the same way) are used during the summers. These weather statistics are used to measure how cold (or warm) a given period has been, and they are also central in calculating for heating-oil deliveries (see page 67).

Extension Activities

• Local news station meteorologists love to visit schools and do presentations.

• This type of chart project would be a good opportunity for students to collect their own data and calculate the information.

Answers

Date	Hi Temp	Lo Temp	Degree Days	Total Degree Days
2/1/98	24°	20°	43	43
2/2/98	27°	18°	42.5	85.5
2/3/98	29°	22°	39.5	125
2/4/98	34°	25°	35.5	160.5
2/5/98	33°	21°	38	198.5
2/6/98	27°	19°	42	240.5
2/7/98	26°	12°	46	286.5
2/8/98	28°	18°	42	328.5
2/9/98	30°	20°	40	368.5
2/10/98	35°	24°	35.5	404
2/11/98	39°	30°	30.5	434.5

Date	Hi Temp	Lo Temp	Degree Days	Total Degree Days
2/12/98	44°	32°	27	461.5
2/13/98	42°	31°	28.5	490
2/14/98	36°	27°	33.5	523.5
2/15/98	29°	5°	48	571.5
2/16/98	25°	-2°	53.5	625
2/17/98	27°	10°	46.5	671.5
2/18/98	32°	16°	41	712.5
2/19/98	36°	22°	36	748.5
2/20/98	40°	28°	31	779.5
2/21/98	28°	7°	47.5	827

10. Heating Degree Days

Paul Cousins is a TV meteorologist. As well as predicting the coming weather, Paul keeps statistics on past weather. One statistic he keeps is heating degree days. Paul calculates heating degree days by finding the average of the high and low temperature for a given day and then subtracting it from 65°. Paul uses this number to show people how cold it has been and also to help heating-oil companies plan their deliveries. Paul has kept the following table of high and low temperatures for the first three weeks of February. Can you help him finish calculating the number of heating degree days each day and the running total for the month?

Date	Hi Temp	Lo Temp	Degree Days	Total Degree Days
2/1/98	24°	20°	_____	_____
2/2/98	27°	18°	_____	_____
2/3/98	29°	22°	_____	_____
2/4/98	34°	25°	_____	_____
2/5/98	33°	21°	_____	_____
2/6/98	27°	19°	_____	_____
2/7/98	26°	12°	_____	_____
2/8/98	28°	18°	_____	_____
2/9/98	30°	20°	_____	_____
2/10/98	35°	24°	_____	_____
2/11/98	39°	30°	_____	_____
2/12/98	44°	32°	_____	_____
2/13/98	42°	31°	_____	_____
2/14/98	36°	27°	_____	_____
2/15/98	29°	5°	_____	_____
2/16/98	25°	-2°	_____	_____
2/17/98	27°	10°	_____	_____
2/18/98	32°	16°	_____	_____
2/19/98	36°	22°	_____	_____
2/20/98	40°	28°	_____	_____
2/21/98	28°	7°	_____	_____

11. Batting Average

Goal

To put the concept of rates into a sports context (batting average) that is familiar to students

NCTM Standards Addressed

Standard 1: Mathematics as Problem Solving

Standard 2: Mathematics as Communication

Standard 4: Mathematical Connections

Standard 6: Functions

Standard 10: Statistics

Teaching Notes

A rate is usually an amount of work accomplished in a given period. Some rates, however, are not stated "_____ per _____." For example, in baseball, a player's batting average is really a rate. It tells you the rate of hits a batter gets per official at-bat. The batting average is calculated by taking the number of hits a batter gets and dividing it by the number of official at-bats (opportunities) he or she has. When a batter is walked, hit by a pitch, or sacrifices (bunts or flies out to the team's benefit), it does not count as an official at-bat. The formula for batting average is hits/official at-bats.

Context

The questions in this section were all researched using the *Baseball Encyclopedia*. Most baseball fans love to discuss and manipulate statistics, and batting average is a popular one.

Extension Activities

The *Baseball Encyclopedia* is an excellent resource for baseball statistics going back more than a century. Encourage students to search this book, a current newspaper, or even get statistics on a school team to prepare several questions like those included in the handout.

Answers

1. Duffy's amazing 1894 batting average was .440.

2. Dropo's career batting average was .270.

3. Ruth had 42 hits in World Series play.

4. Ferguson had 91 hits in 1878.

5. Versalles had 667 at-bats in 1965.

6. Gwynn had 419 at-bats in 1994.

7. Cobb batted .240 in his only bad year.

8. The DiMaggio Brothers' combined batting average for 1940 was .318.

9. Robinson had 589 at-bats in his first season in the majors.

11. Batting Average

Baseball statistics have become a big business, as you can tell by the number of publications about baseball stats that start appearing on the bookstore racks each January. Marc works for a baseball statistics firm that publishes historical and current almanacs of statistics. Recently, his researchers provided him with the following data about batters and their batting averages. They left some work for Marc to do in calculating some of the statistics. Marc knows that in baseball a player's batting average is actually the rate of hits per official at-bats. Official at-bats exclude when a batter is walked, hit by a pitch, or sacrifices (bunts or flies out to their team's benefit). Marc calculates a player's batting average by dividing the player's hits by his/her official at bats. Marc could use help with the following calculations:

1. In 1894, Hugh Duffy, a center-fielder for the Boston Nationals, had the best season for batting average in history. He led the league with 237 hits in 539 official at-bats. What was his batting average in this historic season?

   _____

2. Walt "Moose" Dropo had a 13-year major league career with the Red Sox, Tigers, White Sox, Reds, and Orioles. In his career, he batted 4,124 times and recorded 1,113 hits. What was Dropo's career batting average?

   _____

3. George Herman "Babe" Ruth was arguably the greatest hitter of all time. He played in 10 World Series with the Red Sox and Yankees, batting .326 in 129 at-bats in the series. How many hits did Ruth have in the World Series?

   _____

4. Robert Vavasour "Death to Flying Things" Ferguson had his best batting year with the Chicago Nationals in 1878. He had a batting average of .351 in 259 at-bats. How many hits did he have?

   _____

(continued)

11. Batting Average *(continued)*

5. In 1965, Zoilo Versalles of the Minnesota Twins led the league in official at-bats. He had a batting average of .273, knocking out 182 hits. How many official at-bats did he have?

   _____

6. Tony Gwynn is considered one of the greatest hitters of the modern era. During the strike-shortened 1994 season, he had his highest batting average ever, accumulating 165 hits and a .394 batting average. How many at-bats did Gwynn have in this season?

   _____

7. Tyrus Raymond "Ty" Cobb has the highest career batting average ever. In his 24-year career, he batted below .300 only once! It was his first year in the majors and he had 36 hits in 150 at-bats. What was Cobb's career-low batting average in 1905?

   _____

8. Dom, Joe, and Vince DiMaggio were undoubtedly the greatest set of three brothers to play in the majors. In 1940, Dom had 126 hits in 418 at-bats, Joe had 179 hits in 508 at-bats, and Vince knocked out 104 hits in 360 at-bats. What was the DiMaggio family batting average in 1940?

   _____

9. In 1947, John Roosevelt "Jackie" Robinson broke the color barrier in the major leagues. Despite the pressures of the season, Robinson rapped out 175 hits and batted .297. How many at-bats did he have in 1947?

   _____

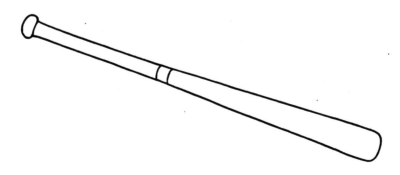

12. Slugging Average

Goal

To put the concept of rates into a sports context (slugging average) that is familiar to students

NCTM Standards Addressed

Standard 1: Mathematics as Problem Solving

Standard 2: Mathematics as Communication

Standard 4: Mathematical Connections

Standard 6: Functions

Standard 10: Statistics

Teaching Notes

In baseball, a player's "slugging average" is really a rate. It tells you the number of bases a batter earns per official at-bats. An official at-bat is recorded whenever a batter gets up and does not get a walk, get hit by a pitch, or hit into a sacrifice (intentional) out. The formula for slugging average is

$$\frac{[\text{No. of singles} + 2 \times (\text{No. of doubles}) + 3 \times (\text{No. of triples}) + 4 \times (\text{No. of home runs})]}{\text{Number of official at-bats}}$$

Context

The questions in this section were all researched using the *Baseball Encyclopedia*. Most baseball fans love to discuss and manipulate statistics, and slugging average is sometimes a confusing one.

Extension Activities

The *Baseball Encyclopedia* is an excellent resource for baseball statistics going back more than a century. Encourage students to search this book, a current newspaper, or even get statistics on a school team to prepare questions like those included in the handout.

Answers

1. Ruth's best-ever slugging average was .847.

2. Rodriguez had a .408 slugging average in 1995.

3. Maranville's 1919 slugging average was .377.

4. Mellilo's 1931 slugging average was .407.

5. Parker has a career World Series slugging average of .415.

6. Gehrig's career slugging average was .632.

7. All of Reilley's 13 hits were singles.

8. Meixell's hit was a single.

12. Slugging Average

Marc has made a name for himself in the baseball statistics business, but his researchers keep giving him incomplete information. This time he is studying the slugging average, which is calculated by taking the number of bases that a slugger achieves through hitting (singles count as one, doubles as two, etc.), and dividing by the number of official at-bats (opportunities) he or she has. When a slugger is walked, hit by a pitch, or sacrifices (bunts or flies out to the team's benefit), it does not count as part of either total. The formula for slugging average is:

$$\frac{[\text{No. of singles} + 2 \times (\text{No. of doubles}) + 3 \times (\text{No. of triples}) + 4 \times (\text{No. of home runs})]}{\text{Number of official at-bats}}$$

Help Marc complete the following slugging average data:

1. Babe Ruth owns six of the top-10 all-time highest slugging averages for a year. In 1920, he set the record for highest slugging average for a season ever when he hit 54 home runs, 9 triples, 36 doubles, and 73 singles in his 458 at-bats. What was his slugging average in this historic season?

_____

2. Alex Rodriguez, the star shortstop for the Seattle Mariners, had 142 at-bats in 1995. He hit 20 singles, 6 doubles, 2 triples, and 5 home runs. What was his 1995 slugging average?

_____

3. Walter James Vincent "Rabbit" Maranville was a star for the Boston Braves. In 1919, he knocked out 95 singles, 18 doubles, 10 triples, and 5 home runs. If he had 480 official at-bats, what was his slugging average?

_____

4. Oscar Donald "Spinach" Mellilo was a regular with the 1931 St. Louis Browns. In 617 at-bats that year, he hit 142 singles while bashing 34 doubles, 11 triples, and 2 home runs. What was his slugging average for the 1931 season?

_____

(continued)

33 *Real-Life Math: Fractions, Ratios, and Rates*

12. **Slugging Average** (continued)

5. David Gene "The Cobra" Parker went to the World Series three times, in 1979 with the Pittsburgh Pirates, and again with the Oakland Athletics in 1988 and 1989. In his World Series career, Parker batted 53 times, getting 10 singles, 4 doubles, and 1 home run. What was his World Series slugging average?

_____

6. Henry Louis "Lou" Gehrig held the record for consecutive games played until it was broken in 1996 by Cal Ripken, Jr. Before his career and life were cut short by ALS (amyotrophic lateral sclerosis), Gehrig had 8,001 at-bats, hitting 493 home runs, 162 triples, 535 doubles, and 1,531 singles. He finished third on the all-time career list with what slugging average?

_____

7. Alexander Aloysius "Duke" Reilley wasn't very big (his teammates called him "Midget"). He played 20 games in 1909 for Cleveland. In his 62 at-bats he had 13 hits. His slugging average was .210. How many singles did Reilley hit?

_____

8. Merton Merrill "Moxie" Meixell played only two games in the major leagues, both with the 1912 Cleveland Spiders. He had two at-bats and one hit. His career slugging average was .500. What kind of hit did he get?

_____

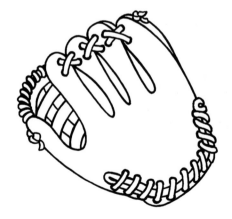

13. Hard Disk Drive Speeds

Goal

To get a sense of calculating with rates relating to information storage and spinning speeds of disk drives

NCTM Standards Addressed

Standard 1: Mathematics as Problem Solving

Standard 2: Mathematics as Communication

Standard 4: Mathematical Connections

Standard 5: Algebra

Standard 6: Functions

Teaching Notes

The calculations on this sheet are based on the formula for the circumference of a circle, $C = 2\pi r$. One revolution will bring $2\pi r$ inches of information past the reader. The density of the packing of bits of information varies by machine and type of disk.

Context

Computer disk drives, disks, and readers carry immense amounts of information. The speed with which the information is read determines whether it is possible to complete certain types of projects. A videographer, for instance, has a series of pictures, each of which require large amounts of information space.

Extension Activities

Computer technology changes so rapidly that even experts can get confused by all the variations on concepts. A local programmer might come in to talk with students about how calculation speed and reading speed affect most people's activities. Some of your students may know enough about this to do a presentation.

Answers

1. 17,270 bits fit on the outermost edge of this disk.

2. 7,850 bits fit on the innermost track of the disk.

3. The reader would read 785,000 bits in 20 seconds.

4. The reader would read 1,295,250 bits in 15 seconds.

5. The reader must range from 39,250 bps to 86,350 bps.

6. The reader must be capable of 91,583 bps in this configuration.

13. Hard Disk Drive Speeds

Dom is a videographer. He films with a video camera and then downloads the film onto his computer, where it is stored electronically on the hard drive. He then edits it using his computer. The problem is that information stored toward the outer edge of a 5½" disk spins past the reader much faster than information stored at the inner edge. Readers must be taught to gather information at different speeds. Dom is shopping for a new disk drive. Using the formula $C = 2\pi r$ ($\pi = 3.14$), help Dom evaluate some new models.

1. Dom is looking at a 5½" disk drive. It writes information at a rate of 1 bit per .001 inches. How many bits of information will fit on the outermost edge of the disk?

   _____

2. The center of a disk isn't writeable; only the outer 1½" can be read. How many bits of information will fit on the innermost writeable track of the above disk?

   _____

3. The drive Dom is considering buying spins at 300 rpm. How much information would the reader read at the inner edge of the disk in 20 seconds?

   _____

4. How much information would the drive read at the outer edge of this disk in 15 seconds?

   _____

5. Given your answers to questions 3 and 4, what range of speeds must the reader have in bits per second?

   _____

6. New technology has come out with a 3½" disk that spins at 500 rpm. What is the maximum bits per second reading speed necessary for this disk and drive?

   _____

14. Exercise and Calories

Goal

To learn about rates in the context of exercise and burning calories

NCTM Standards Addressed

Standard 1: Mathematics as Problem Solving

Standard 2: Mathematics as Communication

Standard 4: Mathematical Connections

Standard 5: Algebra

Standard 6: Functions

Teaching Notes

Two factors go into calculating the number of calories a runner burns while running on a flat surface: the weight of the runner and the speed and length of time he or she is running. The formulas for these calculations are (1) $K = \frac{1}{8}W - \frac{3}{4}$ and (2) $C = KD$, where K is the number of calories burned per mile of running, W is the weight of the runner (in kilograms), C is the number of calories burned, and D is the number of miles run.

Context

Our society is very conscious of exercise for health and fitness. The body keeps its energy up by burning calories. When a person runs on a flat surface, he or she burns calories

at a relatively constant rate. Running faster shortens the workout, but running five miles in 30 minutes doesn't burn more calories than running five miles in an hour—it just burns them in less time.

Extension Activities

- Many physiology texts include information about energy expenditure and calories. Students could research other forms of exercise and the numbers involved in those forms.

- Newer exercise machines have computers that calculate the calories burned in a period of exercise. Sample numbers from these machines could be used to build equations for that form of exercise.

Answers

1. Samír will burn 119 calories per mile.

2. Tyler will burn 400 calories in his run.

3. Lori ran 6.87 miles.

4. Unice will burn 93 calories per mile.

5. Terrence would burn 289 calories in her run.

6. Natasha ran 8.7 miles.

7. Chris weighs 70 kg.

14. Exercise and Calories

Katie Hall is a personal trainer. She assists individuals in setting up healthy exercise patterns and sticking to them. Good health is a combination of sufficient and safe exercise and good nutrition. For their exercise programs, Katie advises many of her clients to run on a flat surface. She makes recommendations about how fast and how far they should run for them to exercise safely. Katie also determines the number of calories that a client will burn during their run.

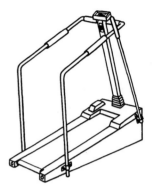

The formulas for these calculations are $K = 13/8\ W - 5/4$ and $C = KD$ where K is the number of calories burned per mile of running, W is the weight of the runner (in kilograms), C is the number of calories burned, and D is the number of miles run. Can you help Katie calculate the data she needs for the following clients?

Some of Katie's new clients require advice about how far and how fast they should run under the following circumstances. (Round answers to the nearest tenth.)

1. Samír weighs 74 kg. How many calories per mile did Katie calculate that he will burn in running on a flat surface?

_____

2. Tyler weighs 50 kg. How many calories did Katie calculate that he will burn in a 5-mile run?

_____

3. Lori weighs 52 kg. She burned 572 calories in her run yesterday. How far did she run?

_____

4. Unice weighs 58 kg. How many calories per mile will she burn in running on a flat surface?

_____

5. Terrence weighs 60 kg. How many calories would she burn in a 3-mile run?

_____

6. Natasha weighs 58 kg. She burned 810 calories in her run yesterday. How far did she run?

_____

7. Katie works with Chris Cyll, a cross-country runner. In yesterday's workout, Chris ran 9⅓ miles. She calculated that he burned 1,050 calories. How much does Chris weigh?

_____

15. Tipping

Goal

To learn about calculating tips or gratuities in restaurants, from the server's point of view

NCTM Standards Addressed

Standard 1: Mathematics as Problem Solving

Standard 2: Mathematics as Communication

Standard 4: Mathematical Connections

Teaching Notes

Rates are often given in percentages. To calculate a tip, you simply multiply the food bill (usually before taxes are added) by the percentage of tip you want to leave: food bill × percent = tip. Of course, this formula can be manipulated to calculate the size of the bill or the percent that the tip represents of that bill. You may want to discuss the wage structure for servers (below minimum wage base + tips) so that students understand the importance of tips. An explanation of the reason for restaurant's policy about large parties might also be helpful.

Context

Almost everyone eats in a restaurant at some point, and we usually leave a tip for the server. For states where the restaurant tax is 8 percent, many people just double the tax (or triple a 5 percent tax). In some metropolitan areas, expected tips have gone up to 20 percent in recent years.

Extension Activities

Students can interview restaurateurs and service staff at local restaurants to learn more about tips. They can also brainstorm lists of other professions where employees receive tips.

Answers

1. Dalit added a $17.03 gratuity to the bill.

2. The anniversary couple's tip represented 17.5 percent of the food bill.

3. The businesswoman left a $3.11 tip.

4. The gentleman's tip represented 10.8 percent of his food bill.

5. Dalit charged the birthday party a $33.52 gratuity.

15. Tipping

Dalit has a great job as a server at an upscale restaurant. She takes orders, serves food, and ensures a pleasant dining experience for patrons at the table in her station. According to restaurant policy, if there are six or more people in a party, Dalit has to add on a 15 percent gratuity (tip) to the bill before taxes. If a table has five or fewer patrons, they may choose how much they would like to tip. The standard tip used to be 15 percent. However, many people now tip between 20 and 25 percent, depending on the quality of the service they receive. Tips are very important to servers because their hourly wage is about half of minimum wage. Fortunately, Dalit is good at her job!

To calculate a tip, you simply multiply the sum of the food and beverage bill (before sales tax is added) by the percentage of the tip you want to leave: food sum × percent = tip.

Answer these questions about Dalit's tip income from last Friday night:

1. Dalit's first table was a family of seven. Everyone had sodas, salads, and entrees. Their bill came to $113.52. Dalit had to calculate the gratuity to include in the bill. How much gratuity did she include?

   _____

2. Dalit also served a couple celebrating their anniversary. They had a bottle of champagne, hors d'oeuvres, salads, entrees, dessert, and coffee. Their bill was for $85.63 before tax, and they tipped $15.00. What percent of their food bill did the tip represent?

   _____

3. Dalit served a businesswoman, dining alone, who just wanted some soup, salad, and water. Her bill came to $12.43. She appreciated that Dalit was friendly and efficient and wanted to tip 25 percent. How much of a tip did she leave?

   _____

4. A fussy gentleman came in and ordered several items that were not on the menu. Unfortunately, one of the bus-people also spilled the gentleman's water while pouring it for him. The diner felt that he didn't get good service, and he left only a $2.00 tip on a bill of $18.50. What percent tip was this?

   _____

5. Four couples came in together to celebrate someone's birthday. Dalit did her best to keep them happy but also to keep them quiet enough that they didn't disturb her other diners. They ate a lot, running up a bill of $223.45. How much gratuity did Dalit charge them?

   _____

16. Produce, Meats, and Cheeses

Goal

To learn how to calculate with rates, using produce and deli prices in a grocery store

NCTM Standards Addressed

Standard 1: Mathematics as Problem Solving

Standard 2: Mathematics as Communication

Standard 4: Mathematical Connections

Standard 5: Algebra

Standard 6: Functions

Teaching Notes

Perhaps the most common rate NOT related to speed or work is "price per pound." Many everyday items are purchased by the pound. To determine the price of an item, you weigh it and then multiply the weight in pounds by the price per pound. The formula is

price = no. of pounds × price per pound.

Context

Grocery stores are valuable sources of math problems. Nearly every item in the produce, deli, and meat sections of a grocery store has prices given by the pound. As students learn to shop and estimate, they will begin to see differences in prices and become better mathematicians and more careful shoppers, too.

Extension Activities

Grocery stores are usually willing to have small groups visit on field trips. Students can learn about pricing of produce, meats, and cheeses, and how scales are used in pricing items.

Answers

Item	Weight	Price/ Pound	Cost
American cheese	6 ounces	2.59	0.97
Bananas	2.38 pounds	0.29	0.69
Bologna	.67 pounds	2.09	1.40
Bosc pears	.80 pounds	0.79	0.63
Broccoli crowns	10 ounces	0.89	0.56
Brussels sprouts	.44 pounds	0.65	0.29
Capacola	4.5 ounces	4.19	1.18
Green beans	.54 pounds	1.49	0.80
Green cabbage	1.08 pounds	0.19	0.21
Hamburger	3.44 pounds	1.29	4.44
Lobster	1.33 pounds	5.99	7.97
Pea pods	.22 pounds	2.29	0.50
Pork chops	2.12 pounds	1.59	3.37
Red peppers	.45 pounds	1.99	0.90
Salad bar	.96 pounds	3.19	3.06
Swiss cheese	5 ounces	4.99	1.56
Swordfish steak	1.85 pounds	6.99	12.93
Tomatoes	.32 pounds	1.79	0.57
Turkey ham	.49 pounds	2.49	1.22
Yellow turnip	.55 pounds	0.39	0.21

16. Produce, Meats, and Cheeses

Joelle is a careful shopper. She keeps track of how much she spends and whether an item is within her price range. Joelle likes fresh produce, meats, and cheeses, all of which are sold at a given "price per pound." On a recent trip to the store, Joelle came across the following prices and weights. Calculate how much Joelle spent on each item below:

Item	Weight	Price per pound	Cost
American cheese	6 ounces	2.59	_____
Bananas	2.38 pounds	0.29	_____
Bologna	.67 pounds	2.09	_____
Bosc pears	.80 pounds	0.79	_____
Broccoli crowns	10 ounces	0.89	_____
Brussels sprouts	.44 pounds	0.65	_____
Capacola	4.5 ounces	4.19	_____
Green beans	.54 pounds	1.49	_____
Green cabbage	1.08 pounds	0.19	_____
Hamburger	3.44 pounds	1.29	_____
Lobster	1.33 pounds	5.99	_____
Pea pods	.22 pounds	2.29	_____
Pork chops	2.12 pounds	1.59	_____
Red peppers	.45 pounds	1.99	_____
Salad bar	.96 pounds	3.19	_____
Swiss cheese	5 ounces	4.99	_____
Swordfish steak	1.85 pounds	6.99	_____
Tomatoes	.32 pounds	1.79	_____
Turkey ham	.49 pounds	2.49	_____
Yellow turnip	.55 pounds	0.39	_____

17. Unit Pricing

Goal

To use rates in the familiar concept of unit pricing of groceries

NCTM Standards Addressed

Standard 1: Mathematics as Problem Solving

Standard 2: Mathematics as Communication

Standard 4: Mathematical Connections

Teaching Notes

A rate is usually an amount of work or accomplishment achieved in a given period. It is generally given as "_____ per _____." It can also be a value for a certain amount of time or money. We can talk about "miles per hour," "goals per game," "dollars per hour," or "dollars per pound." In the case of unit pricing, the idea is to get a comparative price between two items of different size and price. The formula for calculating price per ounce is

cost of package/size of package (in ounces) = cost per ounce.

Context

Most of us shop in grocery stores at least periodically. So many people now comparison shop that stores advertise their unit prices. As part of budgeting the family money, students should know how to comparison shop.

Extension Activities

Your local grocery store is a wonderful resource for learning unit pricing. The management may be willing to give you a tour and discuss their procedures, or you can suggest that students go to the store and compare the prices on some products. Have them ask why larger containers tend to cost less per unit.

Answers

1. Head and Shoulders™ is cheaper @ 13.5 cents per ounce.

2. The loose carrots @ 35 cents per pound are cheaper.

3. The 10-pound sack @ 12.9 cents per pound.

4. The 20-pound bushels are cheapest @ 84 cents per pound.

5. The 42-ounce bottle is cheaper @ 17.8 cents per ounce.

6. The frozen lemonade is cheapest @ $1.17 per gallon.

7. Debba should buy six 8-ounce bags, costing $9.54.

8. Breda should buy the 64-ounce can for 23.7 cents per ounce.

17. Unit Pricing

Most of us are very careful when we go to the grocery store. We want to save money and still buy what we want. Because of this, most grocery stores now have "unit pricing" on their shelves, so you can compare costs. For instance, a box of Cleano Soap may sell for $1.45, and a box of Scrubbie Soap may cost $2.15. However, if the Cleano Soap box contains 12 ounces, while the Scrubbie Soap box contains 20 ounces, Scrubbie may be a better buy. If you calculate the "price per ounce," you may find that it is more economical to buy the more expensive, but bigger, box.

Help the following careful shoppers choose the best value:

1. Drew wants some new shampoo. He notices that Head and Shoulders™ costs $3.24 for a 24-ounce bottle, and Tegrin™ costs $2.89 for a 19-ounce bottle. If Drew wants to spend as little as possible to get a good shampoo, which brand should he buy?

   _____

2. Noma is deciding whether she should buy her carrots loose or in a 3-pound bag. The loose carrots cost 35 cents per pound and a 3-pound bag of carrots is $1.10. Which should she buy?

   _____

3. Marcus is buying flour to bake bread. He can buy flour in a 5-pound sack, a 10-pound sack, or a 20-pound sack. The 5-pound sack is $.70, the 10-pound sack is $1.29, and the 20-pound sack is $2.75. Which sack represents the best deal?

   _____

4. Betsy loves to can tomatoes. At the corner stand, she can buy a 2-pound package for $1.98, a 5-pound package for $4.75, and a 20-pound bushel for $16.80. Assuming that she wants 40 pounds of tomatoes, what size packages should she buy?

   _____

5. Mr. Neilan thinks olive oil is good for his health. He is willing to buy big jars, because it doesn't go bad on his shelf. Golden Olive has a 17-ounce bottle for $3.29 and a 42-ounce bottle for $7.48. Which bottle should he buy to pay the least amount per ounce?

   _____

(continued)

17. Unit Pricing (continued)

6. Lowell likes lemonade. He can buy a 1-gallon (128-ounce) jug of lemonade for $1.29. He can also buy frozen lemonade concentrate for $0.55, which makes 60 ounces, or powdered lemonade that makes 2 gallons (256 ounces) for $2.89. Lowell knows that he will finish whatever size container he buys. Which container should he buy?

_____

7. Debba is making pizzas. She needs to choose among three bags of shredded mozzarella. One contains 8 ounces and costs $1.59. One contains 12 ounces and costs $2.49. One contains 16 ounces and costs $3.29. If Debba needs 48 ounces of cheese for her pizzas, how many of which type of bag should she buy?

_____

8. Breda is buying wallpaper remover for her bedroom. She learns that the hardware store carries three sizes of cans, 15 ounces for $4.29, 33 ounces for $8.16, and 64 ounces for $15.19. She wouldn't mind having some left over if she doesn't use it all, so which size can should she buy?

_____

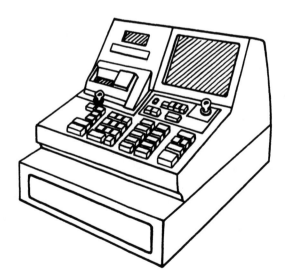

18. Rate of Pay

Goal

To get a sense of calculating with time and rates of pay

NCTM Standards Addressed

Standard 1: Mathematics as Problem Solving

Standard 2: Mathematics as Communication

Standard 4: Mathematical Connections

Standard 6: Functions

Teaching Notes

The difficulties here lie in calculating how much time a person has worked each day, adding those numbers, and then multiplying by a decimal rate. Some students will assume that they can use their calculator to find hours worked, and for a shift from 9:05 A.M. to 3:35 P.M. will put the operation 9.05 – 3.35 = on their calculator. You may want to have them figure out why this *doesn't* work, and develop a strategy for what might.

Context

Timecards are prevalent, especially in the types of jobs that students hold. Not only do they need to know how to deal with their own cards, but someday they may be in charge and need to complete others' cards.

Extension Activities

If students have hourly jobs, have them work out their own earnings. See if you can get a time clock to display (there may be one in the business or maintenance office at your school).

Answers

1. Carlos worked 7.5 + 7.5 + 7.75 + 7.5 + 7.633 = 37.88 hours to earn $333.34.

2. Anthony worked 7.333 + 7.667+ 7.417 + 7.8 + 7.483 = 37.70 hours to earn $254.48.

3. Mustafa worked 7.583 + 7.583 + 7.533 + 7.833 + 7.783 = 38.32 hours to earn $319.21.

4. Robert worked 7.067 + 6.9 + 6.95 + 7.117 + 7.083 = 35.12 hours to earn $345.93.

5. Judy worked 4.083 + 4.15 + 4.333 + 7.0 + 4.033 = 23.60 hours to earn $244.26

6. Amani worked 4.167 + 4.0 + 4.167 + 4.167 + 4.0 = 20.50 hours to earn $135.30.

7. Gail worked 7.0 + 7.583 + 5.917 + 5.5 + 6.917 = 32.92 hours to earn $534.95.

18. Rate of Pay

Traci is responsible for her company's payroll. She gets timecards from seven employees each week, calculates how many hours they have worked, and then calculates how much they are to be paid, based on their rate of pay.

Calculate how much each of the following employees should be paid:

1. Name : Carlos Monteagudo

Day	Time In	Time Out	Hours Worked
Monday	6:30 A.M.	2:00 P.M.	_____
Tuesday	6:35 A.M.	2:05 P.M.	_____
Wednesday	6:30 A.M.	2:15 P.M.	_____
Thursday	6:32 A.M.	2:02 P.M.	_____
Friday	6:55 A.M.	2:33 P.M.	_____

Total hours worked: _____

Rate of pay per hour: $8.80

Payment due: _____

AMERICAN PAYROLL SERVICES

40.00	10.50		420.00	4200.00	SOC. SEC	17.98	256.37
					MEDICARE	4.21	59.96
					FEDERAL TAX	28.36	291.77
					STATE TAX	5.94	64.84

(continued)

18. Rate of Pay *(continued)*

2. Name: Anthony Moor

Day	Time In	Time Out	Hours Worked
Monday	7:00 A.M.	2:20 P.M.	_____
Tuesday	6:55 A.M.	2:35 P.M.	_____
Wednesday	7:03 A.M.	2:28 P.M.	_____
Thursday	6:45 A.M.	2:33 P.M.	_____
Friday	6:58 A.M.	2:27 P.M.	_____

Total hours worked: _____

Rate of pay per hour: $6.75

Payment due: _____

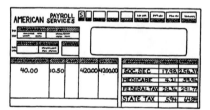

3. Name: Mustafa Khader

Day	Time In	Time Out	Hours Worked
Monday	6:55 A.M.	2:30 P.M.	_____
Tuesday	6:55 A.M.	2:30 P.M.	_____
Wednesday	6:58 A.M.	2:30 P.M.	_____
Thursday	6:45 A.M.	2:35 P.M.	_____
Friday	6:58 A.M.	2:45 P.M.	_____

Total hours worked: _____

Rate of pay per hour: $8.33

Payment due: _____

(continued)

18. Rate of Pay *(continued)*

4. Name: Robert Worley

Day	Time In	Time Out	Hours Worked
Monday	10:06 A.M.	5:10 P.M.	_____
Tuesday	10:08 A.M.	5:02 P.M.	_____
Wednesday	10:10 A.M.	5:07 P.M.	_____
Thursday	10:01 A.M.	5:08 P.M.	_____
Friday	11:00 A.M.	6:05 P.M.	_____

Total hours worked: _____

Rate of pay per hour: $9.85

Payment due: _____

AMERICAN	PAYROLL SERVICES						
40.00	10.50	420.00	420.00	SOC. SEC.	17.98	256.37	
				MEDICARE	4.21	59.96	
				FEDERAL TAX	28.35	291.71	
				STATE TAX	5.94	84.84	

5. Name: Judy Zartman

Day	Time In	Time Out	Hours Worked
Monday	9:00 A.M.	1:05 P.M.	_____
Tuesday	9:05 A.M.	1:14 P.M.	_____
Wednesday	8:55 A.M.	1:15 P.M.	_____
Thursday	6:00 A.M.	1:00 P.M.	_____
Friday	9:02 A.M.	1:04 P.M.	_____

Total hours worked: _____

Rate of pay per hour: $10.35

Payment due: _____

(continued)

18. **Rate of Pay** (continued)

6. Name: Amani Boling-Khader

Day	Time In	Time Out	Hours Worked
Monday	2:00 P.M.	6:10 P.M.	_____
Tuesday	2:05 P.M.	6:05 P.M.	_____
Wednesday	2:08 P.M.	6:18 P.M.	_____
Thursday	2:03 P.M.	6:13 P.M.	_____
Friday	2:07 P.M.	6:07 P.M.	_____

Total hours worked: _____

Rate of pay per hour: $6.60

Payment due: _____

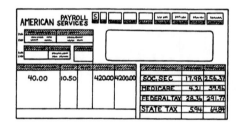

7. Name: Gail Boling

Day	Time In	Time Out	Hours Worked
Monday	7:30 A.M.	2:30 P.M.	_____
Tuesday	10:00 A.M.	5:35 P.M.	_____
Wednesday	10:50 A.M.	4:45 P.M.	_____
Thursday	6:45 A.M.	12:15 P.M.	_____
Friday	7:25 A.M.	2:20 P.M.	_____

Total hours worked: _____

Rate of pay per hour: $16.25

Payment due: _____

19. Population Growth Rates

Goal

To learn about growth rates and population while practicing exponent use

NCTM Standards Addressed

Standard 1: Mathematics as Problem Solving

Standard 2: Mathematics as Communication

Standard 4: Mathematical Connections

Standard 5: Algebra

Standard 6: Functions

Standard 10: Statistics

Teaching Notes

The formula for population growth is fairly easy to derive. Given the rate of growth, r, and the current population (at time zero), P_o, the population after 1 year is given by the formula

$$P(1) = P_o + P_o(r) = P_o(1 + r) \text{ and}$$
$$P(2) = P_o(1 + r) + P_o(1 + r)(r) = P_o(1 + r)^2.$$

Therefore the population at a given time (t) is determined by the formula $P(t) = P_o(1 + r)^t$. This formula is fairly easy for students to manipulate if they know exponents.

Context

Population growth is a global issue because of concerns about whether the earth can sustain a larger population. On a more local scale, population growth and decline has implications for tax structures and representation decisions with respect to local and national government.

Extension Activities

Using almanacs or statistics compendia, students can research, graph, and discover the growth rate of a population. They can then project future population and the political-economic implications of their projections.

Answers

1. Tyler's population will be 18,698 in 2005 at this rate of growth.

2. St. Johnsbury's population will be 6,818 in 2002 at this rate of growth.

3. Evanston's population will be 75,458 in 2003 at this rate of growth.

4. Custer's population will be 5,609 in 2000 at this rate of growth.

5. North Pole's population will be 1,812 in 2010 at this rate of growth.

6. Chicago's population will be 2,453,087 in 2010 at this rate of decline.

19. Population Growth Rates

Whitley Spirer works as a statistician for the U.S. Bureau of the Census. She plots and calculates population changes to determine growth in certain areas and then attempts to project future growth. Her projections are used in setting tax policies and in calculating how many representatives a state or local district may elect. Whitley uses exponents to help her quickly complete her calculations. The formula, with the rate of growth, r, and the current population (at time zero), P, gives the population after one year.
$P(1) = P + P(r) = P(1 + r)$ and $P(2) = P(1 + r) + P(1 + r)(r) = P(1 + r)$. Therefore the population at a given time (t) is determined by the formual $P(t) = P(1 + r)$.

Answer these questions that Whitley has encountered recently.

1. Tyler, Texas, had a population of 16,646 in 1996. They have experienced moderate growth of 1.3 percent per year recently. Katie has been asked to project Tyler's population in 2005. What estimate should Katie give based on past growth?

   _____

2. The population of St. Johnsbury, Vermont, grows at a fairly constant rate of 1.5 percent per year. In 1998, the population is 6,424. What will the population be in 2002?

   _____

3. Evanston, Illinois, has experienced a slow growth rate of .5 percent per year for the last several years. Using this as a model and the knowledge that Evanston's population was 73,233 in 1997, what would you expect to be Evanston's population in 2003?

   _____

4. In 1990 Custer, Idaho, had a population of 4,133. If they have been experiencing an active growth of 3.1 percent per year, what population would you project for the year 2000?

   _____

5. North Pole, Arkansas, had a population of 1,456 in 1990. The population there has grown at a constant rate of 1.1 percent. Approximately how many North Pole inhabitants will there be in 2010?

   _____

6. The city of Chicago had 2,783,726 inhabitants in 1992. Since then they have seen a *decrease* in their population of .7 percent per year. At this rate, how many Chicagoans will there be in 2010?

   _____

20. Half-Life

Goal

To learn about decay rates and half-lives in the context of chemistry while practicing exponent use

NCTM Standards Addressed

Standard 1: Mathematics as Problem Solving

Standard 2: Mathematics as Communication

Standard 4: Mathematical Connections

Standard 5: Algebra

Standard 6: Functions

Standard 10: Statistics

Teaching Notes

The formula for half-life is

$$A(t) = A_0(2)^{-t/h},$$

where A is the amount or concentration of something, A_0 is its original concentration or amount, t is the time since it came into being, and h is its half-life. Because solving for t or h requires logarithms (unless they are obvious), these problems use $A(t)$ and A_0 as the unknowns.

Context

Chemists and physicists figure out decay rates and half-lives of concentrations of chemicals to determine where they are in their life cycles.

Therefore, environmentalists are very concerned with the half-lives of toxins and pollutants, and the rates at which they will decay into (or away from) being dangerous. Similarly, archaeologists often use the Carbon-14 content of an object to determine approximately when it was alive or formed.

Extension Activities

A local museum curator or environmentalist would probably be willing to discuss how they use decay rates. Also, your school's physics or chemistry teacher would probably love to get the chance to address students about this scientific approach in a math classroom.

Answers

1. Carol would expect to find a concentration of 3.04 percent if Professor Campbell is right.

2. When the leak occurred, the toxin's concentration was 42.3 percent.

3. Carol would expect to find a concentration of 1.15 percent if Tad is right.

4. Yes, it is down to 6.2 parts per million.

5. Yes, 2.0×10^{-5} is more than 1.95×10^{-5}, which means the concentration was more than 1 percent at the time of death in 1935.

20. Half-Life

Chemicals and chemical compounds decay steadily over time. Carol Titterton's job involves measuring this decay. She receives samples of various materials from around the world and makes predictions based on her knowledge of half-lives and her chemical analyses. Carol uses the following formula for half lives: $A(t) = A_o(2)^{-t/h}$, where A is the amount or concentration of something, A is its original concentration or amount, t is the time since it came into being, and h is its half life. Carol could use your help to solve the following questions:

1. Professor Campbell has been running an archaeological dig in the Middle East for several years. Some of the dating of the site is tricky. His excavators recently dug up a charcoal fire and he sent Carol a sample. He expects that the charcoal dates from 2100 B.C. Carol knows that the concentration of Carbon-14 in charcoal when it is formed is 5 percent, and that the half-life of Carbon-14 is 5,730 years. If Professor Campbell is right about his dates, about what concentration of Carbon-14 might Carol expect to find in 1998?

_____

2. At a superdump site, a toxin has been leaking for 20 days when an inspector discovers it. Carol knows that the toxin has a half-life of 6 days. The inspector reports that the concentration of the toxin upon discovery is still 4.2 percent in the area. What was the concentration of the toxin when the leak occurred?

_____

3. Tad Baker runs an archaeological dig at a colonial fort. Most of the artifacts that have been found date from after 1725. One day an excavator discovers an old foundation made of oak, which appears to be older. Tad thinks it may date back to 1675. He sends Carol a sample. Carol knows that the half-life of Carbon-14 is 5,730 years and that oak has an initial concentration of 1.2 percent. What concentration of Carbon-14 would Carol expect to find in 1998 if Tad is right about the age of the wood?

_____

4. After a recent oil spill in Portland Harbor, the Environmental Protection Agency (EPA) found that the concentration of oil content in the water was decaying with a half-life of 30 days. The concentration after the spill was 5 parts per thousand. The EPA knows that the water will be safe for all ecological purposes when the concentration reaches 7 parts per million. It has been 290 days since the spill. Is the water safe yet?

_____

5. In 1998, in an effort to solve a murder committed in 1935, the police exhume the body of the victim. They want to see if there is a trace of a poison in the skeleton. They know that the poison decays with a half-life of 7 years. To be fatal, this poison must reach a 1 percent concentration throughout the body. They discover that the poison concentration in the bones is only 2.0×10^{-5} in 1998. Could this poison have killed the victim in 1935?

_____

21. Mortgage Rates

Goal

To learn about interest rates and mortgages, also learning the net present value of an annuity formula

NCTM Standards Addressed

Standard 1: Mathematics as Problem Solving

Standard 2: Mathematics as Communication

Standard 4: Mathematical Connections

Standard 5: Algebra

Standard 6: Functions

Teaching Notes

The net present value formula is hard to derive before precalculus, but students can manipulate the formula, as long as they know how to use exponents. (Use of scientific calculators is recommended for calculating exponents.) The formula is

$$A = R \, (1 - (1 + i)^{-n}) \, / \, i,$$

where A = the present value of the loan (purchase price of the house), R = the monthly payments, i = the monthly interest rate (annual rate divided by 12), and n = the number of months in the loan period (for a 30-year mortgage, n = 360).

Context

Mortgage rates fluctuate slowly over the years. As of this writing, mortgage rates are about as low as they have been in 25 years. When people buy a house or make another major purchase, they often do so by borrowing from the bank and agreeing to make monthly payments on the loan. It is always a shock to discover the high cost of this kind of long-term credit.

Extension Activities

Mortgage rates are listed in local newspapers about once a week. Students can research them and local house prices. Students might also call local banks and loan companies to learn about rates and qualifying for loans. Bankers are often willing to come to the classroom to discuss these and other products. Many students will be taking out student loans in the near future, and they will see that student loan repayment is similar to mortgage loans.

Answers

1. a. The couple will have to pay $880.52 each month.

   b. Their cost would be a whopping $316,987.20!

2. The family's payment will be $1,125.59 each month.

3. The newlyweds can afford a loan of $139,763.97.

4. Payments on a 15-year mortgage—$1,902.56.

   Payments on a 30-year mortgage—$1,540.29.

21. Mortgage Rates

Erica Burns is a mortgage broker. She helps customers determine how much they can afford to spend on a home and what loan program best meets their needs. Erica uses the net present value formula to determine principal and interest payments on her clients' home mortgages. The formula is $A = R (1 - (1 + i)^{-n}) / i$, where A = the present value of the loan (purchase price of the house), R = the monthly payments, i = the monthly interest rate (annual rate divided by 12), and n = the number of months in the loan period (for a 30-year mortgage, $n = 360$).

For example, on a 20-year $75,000 loan at 6.75% interest the monthly payments would be calculated as follows: $75,000 = = R (1 - (1 + (.0675 / 12)^{-240}) / (.0675 / 12) = 131.5159565$. This amount is divided into 75,000 to determine $R = \$570.27$.

Help Erica answer the following questions for her clients:

1 a. A couple has picked a house that they want to buy, and they need to borrow $120,000 to make the purchase. Erica finds them a 30-year mortgage at 8 percent. What will their monthly mortgage payments be?

_____

  b. How much will the couple in problem 1a. end up paying for their house if they make 360 payments of the amount you found?

_____

2. A family of five needs a bigger house. They ask Erica to find them a 30-year mortgage for $165,000 that is affordable. She finds a 7.25 percent mortgage rate for families. How much will their monthly payments be?

_____

3. A pair of newlyweds have carefully budgeted themselves, and calculate that they can afford $1,050 per month in mortgage payments. Erica finds a first-time-buyer loan for 30 years at 8.25 percent. How much can they afford to borrow to buy their house?

_____

4. A young family has recently increased their income and wants to move into a bigger home. They like a house for which they would have to borrow $215,000. Erica offers them a 15-year mortgage at 6.75 percent or a 30-year mortgage at 7.75 percent. What would their monthly payments be on each loan?

_____

22. Auto Loan Rates

Goal

To learn about interest rates and auto-mobile loans, also learning the net present value of an annuity formula

NCTM Standards Addressed

Standard 1: Mathematics as Problem Solving

Standard 2: Mathematics as Communication

Standard 4: Mathematical Connections

Standard 5: Algebra

Standard 6: Functions

Teaching Notes

The net present value formula is hard to derive before precalculus, but students can manipulate the formula, as long as they know how to use exponents. The formula is

$$A = R \, (1 - (1 + i)^{-n}) \, / \, i,$$

where A = the present value of the loan (purchase price of the car), R = the monthly payments, i = monthly interest rate (annual rate divided by 12), and n = the number of months in the loan period (for a 5-year auto loan, $n = 60$).

Context

Many high school students are getting their licenses and have first-time use of a car, either their own or a family member's. Most people who are new to cars think of costs as being the gas and perhaps the insurance. When they are buying a car, they think of the size of the monthly payment, rather than the amount they will ultimately pay.

Extension Activities

Students can approach these exercises as potential car buyers. Local banks and credit unions will discuss terms and potential for credit, and often are willing to send a representative to your classroom.

Answers

1. Eath can afford to pay $4,803.82 for his car.

2. Bethany will pay $142.58 each month, and $5,132.88 altogether.

3. Vernon will pay $305.16 per month. The total cost of the car is $20,309.60, including $18,306 in payments plus $2,000 in down payment.

4. Alex can afford $3,663.28 for her car.

5. Megan will pay $165.33 per month.

6. Katherine can afford to pay $9,355.03 for her car.

22. Auto Loan Rates

So you think you want to buy a car? Cars are expensive tools. In addition to the purchase price, you have to pay for maintenance, gas, insurance, and storage or parking. The size of your monthly payment is an important consideration in buying a car, but so are the total amount you are paying to use credit and ensuring that you never owe more than the car is worth.

Answer these questions about auto loans that might arise in buying a car:

1. Eath Nhonh needs a car to get to his new job each day. He figures he can afford to pay $120 each month. Since he is not looking at a new car, his bank will only give him a 4-year loan, at 9.20 percent interest. Given these parameters, what is the most Eath can afford to pay for a car?

   _____

2. Bethany Ives wants a car because she lives a good distance from her school and most of her friends. She has seen a 1993 Subaru for $4,500. She can get a 3-year loan at 8.75 percent from her parent's credit union. What will her monthly payments be and how much will she end up paying for the car over the 3 years?

   _____

3. Vernon Crump has his heart set on buying a 1997 Toyota RAV4. A dealer near his home has a blue one for $16,495 (plus the 5 percent sales tax in his state). Vernon can afford to pay $2,000 now and must borrow the rest. The dealer is offering him a 5-year loan at 7.25 percent. What will Vernon's payments be and how much will he pay for the car (and tax) over 5 years?

   _____

4. Alex Brinkman-Young has to get a new car because someone hit and destroyed her old one. She feels she can afford to pay $90 each month, and the best loan terms she has found offer her an 8.33 percent interest rate on a 4-year loan. What is the maximum value of the car Alex should be looking for?

   _____

5. Megan Butler would like to trade up for a minivan because she has new twins. She finds a minivan advertised at $10,495.00 (plus 6 percent tax). Her current car is all paid for, but is only worth $4,300.00 in trade. She finds a loan for 4 years at 7.6 percent. What will the monthly payments be?

   _____

6. Katherine Chase needs a car capable of making a long trip. She feels that she can afford to pay $185.00 each month, and the dealer is offering her a 4½-year loan at 2.9 percent. What is the maximum price that Katherine can afford to pay for her car?

   _____

23. A Trip to Canada

Goal

To use conversion factors in switching between length and volume measures in the English and metric measurement

NCTM Standards Addressed

Standard 1: Mathematics as Problem Solving

Standard 2: Mathematics as Communication

Standard 4: Mathematical Connections

Standard 5: Algebra

Standard 6: Functions

Standard 12 (MS): Geometry

Standard 13 (MS): Measurement

Teaching Notes

The conversion factors between English and metric measurements are listed in the Appendix at the back of this book. For students who are already familiar with conversion, a copy of the appendix should be enough to get them going on this handout. For students new to conversions, a discussion of multiplying fractions and conversions would be in order.

Context

The better part of the world's population uses metric measurement, while the United States and Britain continue to use the English measurement system. Many students traveling outside the country are faced with these conversions.

Extension Activities

Students might enjoy putting themselves in the place of a Canadian traveling to the United States. What conversions would they face?

Answers

1. It is 366 miles from Montreal to Toronto, so it will take about 6 hours and 39 minutes.

2. The home run flew 394 feet.

3. Katie should keep her speed at 43 miles per hour.

4. The temperature in Windsor is predicted to be about 53½°F.

5. 1/2 liter is still more than Katie usually drinks (about 16.9 ounces).

6. Windsor to Sudbury is about 475 miles. No, the trip is more than Katie's projected 400 miles per day, so she won't make it.

7. Katie is paying $1.78 (U.S.) per gallon.

23. A Trip to Canada

Jasmin is planning a trip to Canada. The problem is that in Canada, everything is measured using the metric system. She will need to contend with different numbers for speed limits, distances, gasoline fill-ups, temperatures, and container sizes. See if you can help Jasmin on her trip. Use the conversion factors below to help with your calculations.

Conversion Factors

English Length	Metric Length
1 inch	= 2.54 centimeters
.394 inches	= 1 centimeter
1 foot	= 30.48 centimeters
.033 feet	= 1 centimeter
1 yard	= .9144 meters
1.094 yards	= 1 meter
1 mile	= 1.609 kilometers
.622 miles	= 1 kilometer

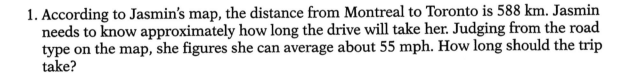

Volume

33.8 ounces	= 1 liter
1 ounce	= .03 liters

Temperature

Fahrenheit	Celsius

Fahrenheit degrees = $\frac{9}{5}$ × (Celsius degrees) + 32

1. According to Jasmin's map, the distance from Montreal to Toronto is 588 km. Jasmin needs to know approximately how long the drive will take her. Judging from the road type on the map, she figures she can average about 55 mph. How long should the trip take?

_____

2. Jasmin stops to see a baseball game in Olympic Stadium in Montreal. She notices that the distances to the outfield fences are listed in meters. A player hits a home run that travels 120 meters. How many feet did it fly?

_____

(continued)

23. A Trip to Canada *(continued)*

3. Jasmin knows that speed limits are listed in kilometers per hour. The speedometer on her car has only miles per hour. When the speed limit in Canada is 70 kph, what speed should Jasmin go?

   _____

4. Jasmin sees on the weather report in Toronto that the weather in Windsor tomorrow is expected to be 12°C. What temperature should she look forward to in getting dressed tomorrow?

   _____

5. Jasmin wants to buy a soft drink at a truck stop. Soft drinks are sold in ½-liter, 1-liter, and 1½-liter cups. If Jasmin is usually satisfied with a 12-ounce can of cola, which cup should she buy?

   _____

6. The trip from Windsor to Sudbury, Ontario is 765 kilometers. Jasmin has set a goal of never traveling more than 400 miles per day. Can she make the trip in one day?

   _____

7. Jasmin stops to buy gas and sees that the price is $0.67 (Canadian) per liter. If $1.00 (Canadian) is worth $0.70 (U.S.), how much is Jasmin paying (in U.S. $) per gallon of gas?

   _____

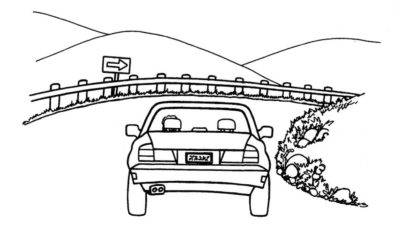

24. Hat Sizes

Goal

To use ratios to create a chart of the relationship between hat sizes and head measurements

NCTM Standards Addressed

Standard 1: Mathematics as Problem Solving

Standard 2: Mathematics as Communication

Standard 4: Mathematical Connections

Standard 5: Algebra

Standard 6: Functions

Standard 7: Geometry From a Synthetic Perspective

Standard 13 (MS): Measurement

Teaching Notes

Hat sizes seem mysterious because they have no obvious connection to the measurements of the head. In fact, the size is determined by a ratio of the circumference of the head in inches divided by 3.14 (π). The formulas for hat size are: hat size = circumference in inches ÷ 3.14 and hat size = circumference in centimeters ÷ 7.98.

Context

Clothing measurements, for example for pants, mention inseam length and waist circumference, and are understandable. Other sizing is less obvious. Most of us wear hats; many of them are adjustable, but some are fitted. The chart on this page could be used in determining hat size.

Extension Activities

Ask students to measure each other's or family members' heads and determine their hat size. Also, ask students to speculate why the formula is what it is. (Early haberdashers used circular forms on which to build hats. Was it easier to identify them by their diameter than by their circumference?)

Answers

Hat Size	Circ. Inches in Decimals	Circumference in Inches	Circumference in Centimeters
6 3/4	21.2	21 1/5"	53.8 cm
6 7/8	21.6	21 3/5"	54.8 cm
7	22	22"	55.8 cm
7 1/8	22.4	22 2/5"	56.8 cm
7 1/4	22.8	22 4/5"	57.8 cm
7 3/8	23.2	23 1/5"	58.8 cm
7 1/2	23.6	23 3/5"	59.8 cm
7 5/8	24	24"	60.8 cm
7 3/4	24.3	24 3/10"	61.8 cm
7 7/8	24.7	24 7/10"	62.8 cm
8	25.1	25 1/10"	63.8 cm
8 1/8	25.5	25 1/2"	64.8 cm
8 1/4	25.9	25 9/10"	65.8 cm
8 3/8	26.3	26 3/10"	66.8 cm
8 1/2	26.7	26 7/10"	67.8 cm

24. Hat Sizes

Many hats are adjustable, but cowboy hats, top hats, dress hats, bonnets, and fitted baseball caps are still sized. Hat size is determined by taking the circumference of the head in inches, and dividing by "pi" (π = 3.14). The conversion of inches to centimeters is 1 inch = 2.54 cm. Using these two pieces of information, hat size can be calculated by dividing circumference in centimeters by 7.98. Hat sizes increase in eighths.

The folks at The Mad Hatter on Congress Street have lost their sizing chart and need a new one for reference. Can you finish filling out the chart below for them?

Hat Size	Circumference Inches in Decimals	Circumference in Inches	Circumference in Centimeters
6¾	_____	_____	_____
_____	_____	_____	54.8 cm
_____	21.6	22"	_____
7⅛	_____	_____	_____
_____	_____	22⅘"	_____
_____	_____	_____	58.8 cm
7½	_____	_____	_____
_____	_____	24"	_____
_____	_____	_____	61.8 cm
7⅞	24.7	_____	_____
_____	_____	25⅒"	_____
_____	_____	_____	64.8 cm
8¼	_____	_____	_____
_____	_____	26³⁄₁₀"	_____
_____	_____	_____	67.8 cm

         Real-Life Math: Fractions, Ratios, and Rates

25. The Musical Scale

Goal

To learn how to work with ratios in the context of the musical scale and string lengths

NCTM Standards Addressed

Standard 1: Mathematics as Problem Solving

Standard 2: Mathematics as Communication

Standard 4: Mathematical Connections

Standard 5: Algebra

Standard 6: Functions

Standard 7: Geometry From a Synthetic Perspective

Standard 13 (MS): Measurement

Teaching Notes

The ratio of string lengths (using strings of constant thickness and makeup) is such that one octave is a ratio of 2:1. The third and fifth steps of the scale are in ratio to the first by 4:3 and 8:5, respectively. Students should measure carefully and maintain constant tension in order to get the proper sound from plucked strings.

Context

The ratio of the lengths of the strings is the way in which many pianos and other stringed instruments are tuned. Other factors include the thickness of the string and the tension on the string. Students who own stringed instruments such as guitars and violins will find that these other methods are used for tuning.

Extension Activities

Encourage students to use clamps and a string of constant thickness and makeup to prepare a stringed instrument capable of playing a major chord. Students might also examine a grand piano; although piano strings are not of constant weight and thickness, the middle octaves are made up of similar types of strings.

Answers

1. The strings should be 42" and 21" in length.

2. The strings should be cut 21", 28", and 33⅓" in length.

3. The high C string is 10" long.

4. The low C string is 21¾" long.

5. The E string in that octave is 30" long.

6. The strings should be 15", 20", 24", and 30" inches long, respectively.

7. The other strings should be 5⅓", 6⅔", 8", 10⅔", 12⅘", and 16".

Name _____ Date _____

25. The Musical Scale

The Pythagoreans, a group of Greek mathematicians and followers of Pythagoras (c. 582–c. 500 B.C.) discovered much of what we know about building our musical scale. Using a piece of thread or string, they could hold the string tight and pluck it to make sounds. They found that if they cut a string 3 cubits long into strings of 1 cubit and 2 cubits exactly, the sound was pleasing to the ear. We refer to this length ratio of 2:1, as an "octave." In a C Major scale, the notes are c,d,e,f,g,a,b,c, and the major chord is c,e,g,c. The Pythagoreans found that the string for G needed to be in ratio to high C as 4:3, and that the length of the E string needed to be in ratio to high C as 8:5.

What lengths should the following strings be to make well-tuned instruments? Remember: The shortest string will make the highest sound.

1. A string of length 63" is to be cut to make strings of one octave difference in sound. How long should each string be?

   _____

2. You have a string of 42" in length that makes a pleasing sound. How long should you cut other strings to make this the low note in a major chord?

   _____

3. The E string on an instrument is 16" long. How long is the high C string?

   _____

4. The G string on an instrument is 14½" long. How long is the low C string?

   _____

5. The G string on another instrument is 25" long. How long is the E string in that octave?

   _____

6. You want to make a four-stringed instrument that will play a major chord. You have a string 89" long. How long should each string be to make your instrument?

   _____

7. You want to make a seven-stringed, major chord, two-octave instrument. The shortest (highest) string is 4" long. How long should the other strings be?

   _____

       Real-Life Math: Fractions, Ratios, and Rates

26. The Respiratory Quotient

Goal

To learn how to work with ratios in the context of physiology and metabolic gas exchange known as the respiratory quotient

NCTM Standards Addressed

Standard 1: Mathematics as Problem Solving

Standard 2: Mathematics as Communication

Standard 4: Mathematical Connections

Standard 5: Algebra

Standard 6: Functions

Standard 10: Statistics

Teaching Notes

The chemical makeup of carbohydrates is $C_6H_{12}O_6$. By adding 6 O_2 molecules, the body creates 6 CO_2 (carbon dioxide) molecules and 6 H_2O (water) molecules. The respiratory quotient then is 6 (CO_2 molecules) ÷ 6 (O_2 molecules) = 1.00.

Context

The respiratory quotient (R.Q.) is calculated by taking the number of CO_2 molecules produced in a metabolic gas exchange and dividing by the number of O_2 molecules consumed to produce that reaction. A rating of 1 (the least oxidation required) comes from a 100 percent carbohydrate. A 100 percent fat requires 23 O_2 molecules to produce 16 CO_2 molecules, and therefore has an R.Q. of .696.

Extension Activities

Students are generally very interested in discussions of nutrition and exercise. Finding a physiologist or nutritionist to come in and discuss these issues can give you many other areas for mathematical discussion. Your school's chemistry teacher may also feel qualified to discuss them.

Answers

1. Pure carbohydrates have an R.Q. of 1.00.

2. Palmitic acid has an R.Q. of 0.696.

3. The protein albumin oxidizes with an R.Q. of 0.818.

4. a. 0.768 liters of CO_2 have been produced.

   b. 3.6 - 0.768 liters = 2.832 liters of CO_2 were produced by converting NON-proteins.

   c. 0.96 liters of O_2 have been consumed.

   d. 4.3 - 0.96 liters = 3.34 liters of O_2 were consumed by converting NON-proteins.

   e. The NON-protein R.Q. is 2.832 ÷ 3.34 = 0.848.

26. The Respiratory Quotient

Kevin Woodhouse is an athlete. He is very concerned with the physiological processes that take place in his body to convert foods to energy. One of these processes is "the respiratory quotient" (R.Q.), a measure of how much oxygen (O_2) is used in converting food to energy. As this metabolic gas exchange takes place, carbon dioxide (CO_2) is produced. The higher the quotient, the higher the carbohydrate content of the food. Lower R.Q.s mean that a food has a higher fat content. The R.Q. is calculated by taking the number of CO_2 molecules produced in a metabolic gas exchange and dividing by the number of O_2 molecules consumed to produce that reaction.

Consider the following information about R.Q. that Kevin has come across.

1. The chemical makeup of carbohydrates is $C_6H_{12}O_6$. By adding 6 O_2 molecules to a carbohydrate molecule, the body creates 6 CO_2 molecules and 6 H_2O (water) molecules. What is the respiratory quotient of this exchange?

   _____

2. The chemical makeup of palmitic acid is $C_{16}H_{32}O_2$. By adding 23 O_2 molecules to a palmitic acid molecule, the body creates 16 CO_2 molecules and 16 H_2O molecules. What is the respiratory quotient of this exchange?

   _____

3. When the body burns proteins, carbon dioxide and water are not the only by-products. The protein albumin $C_{72}H_{112}N_2O_{22}S$ oxidizes with 77 O_2 molecules to produce sulfur trioxide (SO_3), 9 molecules of urea ($CO(NH_2)_2$), 63 molecules of CO_2, and 38 molecules of H_2O. What is the R.Q. of this oxidation?

   _____

4. Most diets are a mixture of carbohydrates, fats, and proteins. However, it is possible to determine the CO_2 produced and the O_2 used in burning proteins by measuring the nitrogen excreted by the body: 1 gram of nitrogen excreted indicates 4.8 liters of carbon dioxide produced by burning proteins. Similarly, 1 gram of nitrogen produced indicates 6.0 liters of oxygen consumed by burning proteins.

   a. If a resting body excretes .16 grams of nitrogen in a 20-minute period, how many liters of CO_2 have been produced by burning proteins?

   _____

   b. We analyzed the expired air coming from this body and found that altogether 3.6 liters of CO_2 were produced. How much was the result of burning NON-proteins?

   _____

   c. In the same test subject, how many liters of O_2 have been consumed by burning proteins?

   _____

   d. In analyzing the expired air, we also find that 4.3 liters of O_2 were consumed. How much was the result of consumption by NON-proteins?

   _____

   e. What is the NON-protein R.Q. of this scenario?

   _____

27. Delivering Heating Oil

Goal

To recognize and practice the use of ratios in a setting such as an oil company's delivery office

NCTM Standards Addressed

Standard 1: Mathematics as Problem Solving

Standard 2: Mathematics as Communication

Standard 4: Mathematical Connections

Standard 5: Algebra

Standard 6: Functions

Teaching Notes

The "k-factor" of a house is the number of degree days since the last delivery divided by the number of gallons delivered. Multiply the k-factor by 176 to get the number of degree days before the ideal next delivery.

Context

Many oil companies have "automatic delivery" customers, to whom they agree to deliver oil on a regular basis all winter. To save on costs, the company wants to deliver as much oil as possible as infrequently as possible. More frequent deliveries of lesser amounts cost the company money that they can't charge customers. However, if they wait too long, the customer will run out of oil (and heat) and likely stop doing business with them. Delivery is based on a calculation of the k-factor of the home, and "heating degree days." Each time a delivery is made, the k-factor of the house is calculated. The k-factor and the number of recent degree days are then used to determine the next delivery date.

Extension Activities

Ask students to research average numbers of degree days for different times of year, and to calculate the k-factor for their own homes.

Answers

1. The k-factor for 844 Belden Avenue is 4.8. Julie should order delivery after about 845 degree days.

2. The k-factor for 5465 South Dorchester is 4.7. Julie should order delivery after about 827 degree days.

3. 181 gallons were delivered to the Kletzien's house on February 5.

4. The k-factor for the Norman's house on Terry Hill Road is 5.1. Julie should order delivery after about 898 degree days.

5. The k-factor for the house at 9810 Kensington Parkway is 5.1. Julie should order delivery after about 898 degree days. (Same answers as exercise 4.)

27. Delivering Heating Oil

Julie is a dispatcher at Howard Oil. She needs to know when her customers will need oil so that she can arrange to have it delivered that day. She figures out when to deliver oil based on heating degree days and k-factors. Each day Julie calls Paul Cousins (her weatherman), who tells her how many heating degree days were recorded the previous day, and she adds it to her running total. The k-factor of a house is the number of degree days since the last delivery divided by the number of gallons delivered. Ideally, Julie would like a driver to deliver 176 gallons of oil per delivery. She determines the ideal delivery date by multiplying the k-factor by 176. Calculate the following information for each house so Julie can plan the next delivery for them.

1. The house at 844 Belden last had a delivery on January 31, 1998. For the last delivery period, 168.4 gallons of oil were delivered after 808 degree days. What is the k-factor for 844 Belden Avenue, and how many degree days should Julie wait for the next delivery?

_____

2. The house at 5465 South Dorchester last had a delivery on January 17th. For the last delivery period, 178.2 gallons of oil were delivered after 833 degree days. What is the k-factor for 5465 South Dorchester, and how many degree days should Julie wait for the next delivery?

_____

3. The last delivery to the Kletzien's house at 319 South Chester Road was made on February 5 after 825 degree days. The computer has recorded a k-factor of 4.55, but the receipt has been lost for the number of gallons delivered. To the nearest gallon, can you tell the Kletzien's how many gallons were delivered on February 5?

_____

4. The last delivery to the Norman's house on Terry Hill Road was made on February 14; 159.3 gallons were delivered. In that delivery period, there were 812 degree days. What is the k-factor for the Norman's house and how many degree days until they should receive a delivery?

_____

5. The last delivery to the house at 9810 Kensington Parkway was made on December 9. For the last delivery period, 165.8 gallons of oil were delivered after 846 degree days. What is the k-factor for 9810 Kensington Parkway and how many degree days should Julie wait for the next delivery?

_____

                             Real-Life Math: Fractions, Ratios, and Rates

28. Packaging and Product Size

Goal

To learn about ratios of sides, area, and volume by working with packaging and advertising in retail settings

NCTM Standards Addressed

Standard 1: Mathematics as Problem Solving

Standard 2: Mathematics as Communication

Standard 4: Mathematical Connections

Standard 5: Algebra

Standard 6: Functions

Standard 7: Geometry From a Synthetic Perspective

Teaching Notes

Given that R_s is the ratio of the sides, R_a is the ratio of the area, and R_v is the ratio of the volumes, the relationship between the sides of two 2-D objects and their areas is $(R_s)^2 = R_a$. Similarly, the relationship between the sides of two 3-D objects and their volumes is $(R_s)^3 = R_v$. Consequently a $3 \times 3 \times 3$ cube contains 27 cubic units of volume, and a $4 \times 4 \times 4$ cube contains 64 cubic units of volume, more than twice as much! Students may need to use manipulatives in building cubes to see this relationship at work.

Context

Packages have become trademarks in our advertising age. If a company's bottle is shaped a certain way and they want to sell a larger bottle, they will probably simply expand the dimensions of the bottle without changing the shape and style. Because small changes in linear size can lead to large changes in volume, it is good to understand the ratios involved.

Extension Activities

Students can go to stores and find examples of larger and smaller packages of the same shape and do an analysis of the volume or area ratios between the packages.

Answers

1. 12" pizza = 113 sq. in., and 14" pizza =153.9 sq. in. A 12" should cost just less than 1.5 times a 10", and a 14" should cost just less than twice a 10".

2. The volume of the can would increase by a factor of 1.73 yielding a 20¾-oz. can

3. The bars now measure 4.7" by 1.4" by .94".

4. The new cans would measure 6.41" tall and 2.14" in diameter.

5. The small pizzas cost 4.7 cents per square inch, and the extra large costs 3.9 cents per inch (a better deal). However, if your party has different tastes, they might prefer separate pizzas with different toppings!

28. Packaging and Product Size

We tend to judge products by their comparative sizes, but sometimes we don't think enough about dimensions. A can that is twice as tall doesn't necessarily hold twice as much. We can make better judgements by comparing the ratio of an object's dimensions to its area or volume. The relationship between the sides of two 2-dimensional objects and their areas can be expressed as $(R_s)^2 = R_a$. The relationship between the sides of two 3-dimensional objects and their volumes is $(R_s)^3 = R_v$. With R_s the ratio of the sides, R_a the ratio of the areas, and R_v the ratio of the volumes. Below are several questions referring to packaging and size of products. See if your estimates are accurate.

1. Have you ever wondered why there seems to be so little difference in the sizes of 10", 12", and 14" pizzas, yet the prices are so different? Calculate the areas of those pizzas and you will see the difference. The number of inches used to describe a pizza is the diameter of the pizza. The area of the pizza is calculated by taking half of the diameter, squaring it and multiplying by "pi" ($\pi = 3.14$). So a 10" pizza has an area of 25π or about 78½ square inches. How many square inches do 12" and 14" pizzas have? What is the ratio of areas for these three pizzas (these would also be the appropriate ratios of prices)?

   _____

2. A 12-ounce soft drink can is approximately 2½" in diameter and 5" in height. In order to maintain the same shape of the can while enlarging it, the company would have to add twice as many inches to the height as to the diameter. If they added ½" to the diameter and 1" to the height, by what factor would they increase the volume?

   _____

3. Several years ago, candy bar makers figured out that consumers would find it more acceptable if they decreased the size of the bars rather than increasing the price. A bar 5" long, 1.5" wide, and 1" thick was decreased from 6 ounces to 5 ounces. What were the new dimensions of the bars?

   _____

4. To save money, a company that cans olives has decided to decrease the size of their cans from 16 ounces to 10 ounces. Because of the distinctive shape of their cans (which are 7½" tall, but only 2½" in diameter), they have decided to maintain the shape but shrink them proportionally. What will the dimensions of the new cans be?

   _____

5. Louie's pizzeria is running a special this month—three small one-topping pizzas for $10.99. A small pizza is 10" in diameter. Louie's also sells an extra-large pizza, which is an 18" pizza with one topping for $9.99. Which order for pizza is a better deal per square inch? Why might you rather order the other option anyway?

   _____

29. Price-Earnings Ratio

Goal

To learn about ratios in the context of price-earning ratios of stocks and how they are used in investment strategies

NCTM Standards Addressed

Standard 1: Mathematics as Problem Solving

Standard 2: Mathematics as Communication

Standard 4: Mathematical Connections

Standard 5: Algebra

Standard 6: Functions

Teaching Notes

The price-earnings ratio of a stock is listed in stock reports in the newspaper each day. The ratio is calculated by taking the closing price per share and dividing it by the reported annual earnings of the company per share of stock.

Context

If you read the stock quotes in the *Wall Street Journal* or comparable publication, there is a great deal of information included about each stock. In one column is the "price-earnings ratio," which is used as part of several stock investment strategies. If the P-E ratio is low, then earnings are high in comparison with the price of the stock. This can mean that the stock is a good deal, or that investor interest is low and the stock price is stagnant.

Extension Activities

The stock quotations are a wonderful source of a variety of comparative and informative data. Students might be asked to follow a stock with a low P-E ratio and another with a high P-E ratio, and see how the prices of those stocks change over a 6- or 8-week period.

Answers

1. IBM is reporting earnings of about $6.17 per share.

2. J.P. Morgan is reporting earnings of about $7.23 per share.

3. MGM Grand has a P-E ratio of 19 right now.

4. UNUM has a P-E ratio of 20 right now.

5. The Disney Company stock is selling at 106.93 per share now.

6. McDonalds stock is selling at 47¼ per share now.

7. Delta Air Lines has a P-E ratio of 9 right now.

8. Texas Instruments is reporting earnings of about $4.55 per share.

Name _____   Date _____

29. Price-Earnings Ratio

Lee Daggett is a personal investment advisor. He sits down with individuals and families and helps them plan their budgeting, spending, saving, and investing for future goals and retirement. One type of investment that Lee has recommended over the years is stocks on the New York Stock Exchange and NASDAQ market. Lee's investment analysts use any number of indicators to predict which stocks will go up in value. One of those predictors is the price-earnings ratio (P-E). The ratio is calculated by taking the closing price per share and dividing it by the reported annual earnings of the company per share of stock. When the ratio of the price per share of a stock over the earnings per share of the company is low, the analysts think it means that investor interest in the stock is low and it will not change much in price. On the other hand, if the P-E ratio is high, the stock may be overvalued.

Answer these questions about price-earnings ratios that Lee has been following recently:

1. IBM stock is selling for 98¾ per share and has a price-earnings ratio of 16. Approximately what are their earnings per share? _____

2. J.P. Morgan Bank stock is selling at 101³⁄₁₆ per share and has a P-E ratio of 14. Approximately what are their earnings per share? _____

3. MGM Grand stock is selling at 35¹³⁄₁₆ per share and reports earnings of $1.88 per share. What is their P-E ratio? _____

4. UNUM stock is selling at 48⅝ per share and reporting earnings of $2.43 per share. What is their P-E ratio? _____

5. The Disney Company is reporting earnings of $2.89 per share. Their P-E ratio is 37. What is the approximate price of a share of Disney stock? _____

6. McDonalds has a P-E ratio of 20 and is reporting earnings of $2.36 per share. What is the approximate price of a share of McDonalds stock? _____

7. Delta Air Lines is reporting earnings of $12.68 per share. Their stock is selling for 114⅛ per share. What is their P-E ratio? _____

8. Texas Instruments stock is selling for 54⅝ per share. The P-E ratio is 12. Approximately what are their reported earnings per share? _____

Share Your Bright Ideas with Us!

We want to hear from you! Your valuable comments and suggestions will help us meet your current and future classroom needs.

Your name_____Date_____

School name_____Phone_____

School address_____

Grade level taught_____Subject area(s) taught_____Average class size_____

Where did you purchase this publication?_____

Was your salesperson knowledgeable about this product?   Yes_____   No_____

What monies were used to purchase this product?

____School supplemental budget   ____Federal/state funding   ____Personal

Please "grade" this Walch publication according to the following criteria:

Quality of service you received when purchasing ....A	B	C	D	F
Ease of use...A	B	C	D	F
Quality of content...A	B	C	D	F
Page layout ....A	B	C	D	F
Organization of material ....A	B	C	D	F
Suitability for grade level ....A	B	C	D	F
Instructional value..A	B	C	D	F

COMMENTS:_____

_____

What specific supplemental materials would help you meet your current—or future—instructional needs?

_____

Have you used other Walch publications? If so, which ones?_____

May we use your comments in upcoming communications?   ____Yes   ____No

Please **FAX** this completed form to **207-772-3105**, or mail it to:

Product Development, J. Weston Walch, Publisher, P.O. Box 658, Portland, ME 04104-0658

We will send you a **FREE GIFT** as our way of thanking you for your feedback. **THANK YOU!**